I Heard a Voice Say, "Never Throw in the Towel"

Linda McCoy and Darien Smith

Darlin Publishing Co.

Published by Darlin Publishin Co.

For more information please contact

Book design by:
Arbor Books, Inc.
www.arborbooks.com

Printed in the United States of America

I Heard a Voice Say, "Never Throw in the Towel"
Linda McCoy and Darien Smith

1. Title   2. Author   3. Memior

Library of Congress Control Number: 2009940046

ISBN 13: 978-0-615-33240-6

I Heard a Voice Say, "Never Throw in the Towel"

Table of Contents

Acknowledgments

Thank you God for giving us favor, wisdom and your strength to endure this long, weary journey with the healthcare system. Thank you to everyone who prayed for us and cried with us during our difficult times. We will always be grateful for all of your prayers, which gave us the strength to fight on.

Thank you, thank you, thank you to all of the healthcare providers who helped us through this process. Special thanks to Heart pharmacy—all of you have been so kind and generous to Darien, providing him with all of his medical supplies and medicines when the insurance company would not pay. Darien is still here because of your kind efforts. We will always be grateful to all of you.

Thank you to Hi-Tech Respiratory Supplies—you all have done the same.

Thank you to all of Darien's nurses. You put in countless hours and made sacrifices beyond the scopes of your jobs to keep my son alive. I love and appreciate all of you; I couldn't have done it without you guys.

Thank you John for your faithfulness and friendship with Darien.

Becky, you are my girl. You have had my back so many times. We love you.

Thank you, CJ, for being a faithful son and brother and for always being there for your brother. I love you, son.

Thank you, CJ Jr., for being a good nephew to your Uncle D and helping take care of him in your own special little way. Me-Ma loves you so much.

Last and not least, thank you, Mama, for being my strength, my motivation and the one I could lean on when all my strength was gone. I love you.

Jerry Goodmark, you are just the wisest man I have ever met. Thank you for putting up with me and understanding our plight. You never gave up on Darien.

God bless you, Dr. Osborne. Thank you for being Darien's physician, friend and protector.

Dr. Marrinson, thank you for keeping my son sane and stable throughout this process. You are a gift from God.

Thank You to all of Darien's other physicians who didn't give up on him and who took on the challenge of keeping him alive—we will always be grateful to all of you.

Aunt Dee, Carolyn, Angela, Alfrieda, Will, Shawn, Jarvis, Ed and Kebba, thank you, thank you, thank you! We love and appreciate all of you.

Thank you, Judge Peter Lopez and Judge Kuker, for your wisdom and guidance throughout this process.

Ted Leopold, God bless you—you are the best!

Gary Farmer, thank you for believing when no one else did, and thank you to all of the other attorneys who worked behind the scenes. To all of the secretaries who put up with me (especially Linda—God knows I appreciate all of your efforts to make all of this a reality), may God bless you all.

Thank you to our co-writer, Jake Brown, and editor James Uttel for making our experience a journey that will never be forgotten.

Special thanks to Marsha Friedman and the entire staff of EMSI public relations company.

Special thanks to John Meddling, photographer.

Mission statement: The purpose and goal of writing this book is to be effective in helping change the laws under the worker's compensation in the US. Our case was helpful in having the laws changed in the state of Florida, but these laws need to reflect each and every state in the US because there are so many people being mistreated by the insurance companies following accidents like my son Darien's, where they're hurt on their jobsites and not thereafter getting the proper medical attention and help they deserve.

Introduction

On May 14, 1972, God blessed me with one of the most precious gifts a mother could ask for: my son, Darien Roosevelt Ma'lik Coley. Fourteen years later, He blessed me with my second-best gift ever, born on my grandmother's birth date, April 29, 1986—Cameron Jerone Clemons. Darien was born on Mother's Day—an extraordinary gift, so he's very, very special. Perhaps an early reflection of the spirit we'd call on often in our life to come together, when Darien came into this world, he came in fighting—literally! When he was born, he came out screaming and actually hit the doctor on the cheek! That inspired our doctor to say, "Oh, my God, we have a little Muhammad Ali!" So he was a fighter from day one! He came into this world raring to go; his spirit was roaring. Still, as a child, Darien was a very quiet kid. He had inner strength but very few words, so he was never a talker. He was always much more of an observer all throughout his adolescence. Even now, he doesn't talk very much, but he observes a lot.

As a child, Darien was immediately well liked by everyone he came into contact with. His school teachers always loved him because of his mild manners. His first love was his third-grade teacher—she was very pretty and just adored Darien. Periodically, I would make surprise visits to the school, watching him through the classroom window. When he came home on those days, I'd tell him what he had done before he could tell me—good or bad. One day, I saw him throw a paper airplane across the room, and when he came home through the door, I told him I'd seen what he'd done. I remember he was so surprised I'd seen him. I replied by telling him that God sees everything, and that He would always let me know. And he believed me, so from then on I had very little disciplinary problems with Darien in elementary school.

Darien was a latch-key kid, and because I would be at work like many single mothers when he got home from school, Darien would have to stay at home alone. He'd always place a call to me at work every day when he arrived home safely, and we always stayed in very close touch during those years. He was a good boy, joining both the Cub Scouts and later the Boy Scouts along with his neighborhood friends, Mark and Magnus, the latter of who still comes around to visit Darien to this day. Another of Darien's friends, Hoppy (a.k.a. William) was like a brother to Darien growing up. Darien spent a lot of time over at Hoppy's house, and his parents would watch over Darien when I was away from home.

Darien learned to fish and hunt lizards with his neighborhood buddies, and he was also close to his cousins, Cam and Junior. Cam taught him how to hunt for birds and how to cook them, as well as how to fight. Junior was his partner in crime, though, when it came to the girls. He is also very close with his female cousins, Harriett, Peaches and Rhonda, and his aunt, Missie. They would all meet up together at Grandma's house every weekend, and she would put them to work. Their code used to be, "Here comes Grandma—LTC." I remember one day I asked him what that meant, and he said, "Looking too comfortable," such that whenever Grandma found anyone sitting too comfortably, she'd find more work for them to do.

***

Darien: Grandma was a very spiritual woman, and I remember she took all of us grandchildren to church every Sunday. At Sunday dinner, she would say grace and make an altar call all at the same time while she was praying—and she still does it to this day: "Lord, please save my children and all my grandchildren,' that has always been her prayer. She was a stern but very sweet woman, and I can see till this day where my mother got so much of her spine and enduring spirit from.

Part I
The Journey

Chapter 1

The God of our Lord, Jesus Christ, the father of Glory, may give you the spirit of wisdom and revelation in the knowledge of him.

—Ephesians 1:17

Darien one year old, 1973

As a kid, Darien loved sports and was especially talented at both football and swimming—he could swim like a fish! I remember he would be in the water swimming, and at the bottom of the pool holding his breath so long I'd be yelling, "Come up!

Come up!" And he'd always emerge from the bottom of the pool with a big smile on his face. So, he was an excellent swimmer and tennis player, but he also ran track, and was also very, very good in weight training. His primary Little League sports were tennis (where he was always MVP), football and track. He'd also taken karate since he was six years old, so as a child there was not a mountain he couldn't tackle. Anything he got involved in, he excelled at, reflective of the fact that Darien has always been a high achiever.

As a child, I remember Darien LOVED Michael Jackson, and had that MH hairdo going on. He could dance just like him and generally speaking was an excellent dancer—I mean, he LOVED to dance, and was even into salsa and taught me how. So from a young age, he used to sing and dance—from the time he was three years old up until his accident. In fact, the last party we went to before Darien's accident, he was singing and dancing, so he always loved to be active. Darien was a sweet boy and would always bring me flowers; from the time he was a little boy playing outside, he would always come home with flowers he'd picked. As a matter of fact, to this day, he still has flowers brought to me. But at a younger age, this told me he was going to be quite the ladies' man as he got into girls and his teenage years.

I was a single mom with Darien from his age of ten on, and was fortunate through my family that Darien had solid, male role models surrounding him. Darien's uncle, Rickey, was his role model in sports. He coached Darien in tennis, track and baseball. It was a blessing because I was a single parent, so I really appreciated the support system we had as a family, and with my neighbors and Darien's teachers. My brother, Brad, (RIP) was Darien's spiritual father and took him under his wings and taught Darien how to be a real man, and I will always appreciate that. Darien loved to listen to his uncle, Ronnie, who played keyboards and introduced him to music. He played an instrumental part in Darien's life in terms of his love for music and dance.

I think it's also important to note that Darien, at the age of thirteen, tried to save his grandfather's life. My father had fallen in the bathroom of my mother's home, and we were homeless at that time and living with my parents. My father had fallen in the bathroom, from a massive heart attack, against the bathroom door, so that we couldn't get to him. Like a little superhero, Darien ran outside and jumped through the bathroom window and got the door open so we could do CPR on him. Though my father didn't make it, it showed what a brave heart my son has had from a young age.

Darien loved his grandfather very much and also had a special bond with his grandmother and to this day, there is nothing they would not do for each other. Darien would give her flowers every week when he saw her, and since his accident, though she's not here with us, she's constantly on the phone, checking in with us. She understood the enormous task that we had before us, and when Darien was at his lowest, at death's door, my mother would fly up here just to walk into his room and sing a song and pray for him. Darien would light up like a Xmas tree; it was and still is magical watching them when they're together.

Grandma and Darien

Chapter 2

My people are destroyed by the lack of knowledge.

—Hosea 4:6

Cameron, eight years old, Little League car wash

Raising Darien, I was very much into black history, and it was very important to me in those days that Darien was educated on his history as an African American. There was a book I bought for and read to Darien called *The Black Book* by Bill Cosby, which was part of my campaign to make sure Darien was educated about everything that black people had discovered and invented. In that era, there was still very little printed in the history books about what black people had accomplished over the years, so I instilled a lot of pride into him, to be proud of his race and his culture, and indeed he is and was.

***

> Darien: It was always important to my mother growing up that I knew about my heritage as an African American, and I remember Muhammad Ali was one of my idols growing up. I also looked up Jesse Owens and Arthur Ashe as role models, as well as Martin Luther King, Jr. I remember always being most inspired by the fight they had in them, and how that determination had helped them achieve so much in their lives. I have been inspired throughout my own struggles and achievements in life by their own.

***

Darien was raised in inner-city Miami, and so as a child, many of Darien's best friends—Johnny and Frankie—were Cuban, so Darien had a very culturally rounded upbringing. In junior high, the weekends were socially reserved for roller skating, movies and Little League, and, of course, running around with his friends. It was very important to me that in the course of that running around, Darien did so with the right crowd, and I did my best to make sure he stayed clear of the gangs in our neighborhood, which thankfully worked because Darien was as put off by drugs as I was. Both of my sons came to me when they first tried marijuana, and I was so thankful because neither one of them liked their experience, and as such, I never had drug problems with either of my sons, and I'm very grateful for that.

In fact, when Darien was thirteen, he'd gone into a recording studio and recorded a rap song called "Crack Monster," and when I want to hear his voice, I play that song. Not surprisingly, Darien listened to a lot of rap back then, but Darien's "Crack Monster" was the only rap song that I ever listened to because I could understand the words and it made sense. Darien listened to 2 Live Crew, and these were very much his afro-wearing and "Santa Clause is a black man" days. It was yet another reflection of how proud Darien grew up to be of his heritage as an African American, and he always believed in himself.

There was a period in our lives when we were homeless, and we went from pillar to post, and when Darien was in high school, I married the wrong man and lost everything I had, including my house, and had to live with different family members. That was the time in his childhood when I really was concerned about Darien turning to drugs, because his friends and everyone around him in the neighborhood were really into drugs, and we were doing really badly. I kept saying to him, "We may not have the material things that everybody has, but we have love," and those years that I spent trying to get back up on my feet was the best time in our life because it brought us closer together. We stuck together, and I told Darien, "No matter what, if we have love, we can conquer anything, and we can make it. Yes, we lost the house, but there are many houses out there." I taught him the value of love and family, and having integrity, and being able to be trusted. I was able to instill that in him at an early age, and thank God he took root to it. He really listened to me. I feel truly fortunate in that area that he did not rebel.

Because we moved around so much, junior high school was a challenge for Darien as he attended several schools, from Indiana to Orlando, Atlanta and Miami, where he finished and graduated from American High School. Throughout much of Darien's childhood, through to now, we always sang songs to lift us when we were facing difficult times. A few come to mind: "The Greatest Love of All," "I Thank You Lord," "The Happy Song" and the O'Jays' "Forever Mine," which was Darien's favorite. Both Darien and his younger brother, CJ, have a love of music; CJ has played piano since the age of four, plays the saxophone, and can tell me the phone number I dial by the tone of each number. I found that amazing, and it was how I knew he was gifted. And while CJ was my musician, Darien is my dancer and my dreamer; he is so smooth on his feet. I can't wait to dance with him again one day…

Darien, fourteen years old

Chapter 3

Now the just must live by faith.

—Hebrew 10:38

Linda, Darien, CJI and CJII, 2008

Darien: My mother indeed raised me to have an unshakable, unmovable faith, and it, along with her support and push, gave me an indomitable spirit to believe in myself that I could do or conquer anything in life. I've always had that faith.

***

From the time I raised Darien, I instilled in him to always stay very positive and always have faith. I think that's the quality that was instilled in Darien that throughout his childhood stood out the most and allowed him to lead and not follow. As a result, he's just always been a strong-willed, determined young man. I remember I used to tell him that I noticed one of his character traits was being stubborn, but rather than as a criticism, I always let him know that I meant it as a good quality—that there was nothing wrong with being stubborn for the *right reasons*.

***

> Darien: Indeed, my mother used to always tell me growing up, "Just make sure you're being stubborn for the RIGHT reasons," and I know that attitude has made a difference in my life.

***

Growing up, Darien always stood his ground and is still standing his ground. The morals and values I taught my sons were simple ones: Love yourself; treat others the way you want them to treat you; if they don't respect you, leave them alone; never put money before people; people are more important than material things; always be honest in all you do because your word is all you have; trust is everything in a relationship; if you can't trust them, leave them alone; give life your best shot; nothing beats the failure but a try; try and try again; and be a godly man. All these values come from my upbringing and church, and my life experience.

I think, most significantly, our relationship with God is what has sustained this family over the years through all our pain, all of our failures and, most importantly, through all of our triumphs that resulted from keeping that faith close to our hearts. To this day, we strive daily to remain humble so we can always be guided in the right direction. I will always say, "Thank you, God, for your faithfulness."

Uncle Ricky McCoy (Darien's Little League coach: tennis, football and baseball)

Chapter 4

Be kindly affectionate one to another with brotherly love in honor of our preferring one another.

—Roman 12:10

CJI and CJII, 2008

I have another son, Cameron Jerone Clemons, nicknamed CJ, who was born when Darien was fourteen. Darien was his father figure and at sixteen stepped up to the plate, and instead of being a big brother wound up being his father figure because he took such an active role in CJ's life, almost literally sometimes to the point of being parental. Darien taught him how to walk and snatched him from under me and said, "You're not gonna make a sissy out of him."

***

> Darien: I remember putting my little brother in Little League, and it definitely toughened him up. Everything that my mother put into me was such a great example in my life that from day one, I turned around and tried to put the same into my little brother.

***

CJ was seven years old when this accident happened, and Darien's accident was very traumatizing to CJ, but to this day, from the time he was a teenager, Darien was his mentor and was determined that CJ was not going to be going the wrong way. So even in his condition, he continued to take CJ under his wing. For instance, every Saturday, Darien and his brother would go down to Shepherd Spinal Center, where they'd "adopted" someone, and would bring them down clothing, food, DVDs, whatever this individual needed. So Darien had CJ right there with him, teaching him how to give, how to be concerned about others who were less fortunate, and I'm very grateful to Darien for taking that role on with his brother. I know it worked, too, because CJ did that for community service for a whole year and a half and still does that at college.

CJ also definitely respects his older brother as a disciplinary figure, because I can fuss at him all day long and he doesn't listen to me, but Darien can say one word to him and he'll jump! I even asked him one day, "Darien is paralyzed, and when he tells you to do something, you respond right away, but when I ask you to do something, you give me a hard time. Why is that?" And I remember it made me smile because he said, "Mom, I'm not crazy. When Darien gets up, he might remember." So CJ has that respect for his brother; his brother is his role model and idol, and when Darien speaks, it's like EF Hutton: That's the last word!

Growing up and seeing his brother stay positive in such adversity has made him very strong. In the early stages of Darien's injuries people could not understand how he could even smile under his circumstances. Still, Darien smiled on, and I could see this was a positive and powerful influence on Cameron, who became thankful for the little things he had. Cameron understands the reason why his brother smiles so much. It is because those who love him the most can see him smile and smile back. There are people who don't appreciate things like walking and talking. That is why seeing Darien go places and watching him tell jokes are more precious than words can express. Cameron aspires to be more like his brother whether it be his sense of humor, his sharp clothes, or his laid-back, cool personality. His brother's condition has taught Cameron many things, but his brother has taught him a lot more.

***

Darien: My brother, Cameron, also admires his mother's unbelievable strength and persistence. We both believe that no one alive, man or woman, could do what my mother has accomplished. I am proud to call her my mother. I love her more than she will ever know.

Uncle Ronnie McCoy (influenced Darien in music)

Chapter 5

I have taught thee in the way of wisdom, I have led thee in right path.

—Prov. 4:11

Darien and CJI, 2008

Throughout high school, Darien was an average student but stood out in sports. He excelled in wrestling and weight training. When Darien was thirteen years old, I took him to the doctor for a checkup and because Darien was small in stature (five feet, nine inches), the doctor recommended at the time that I get him involved in wrestling heading into high school. His doctor had reasoned that if he was involved in wrestling, that would keep him from having that Napoleon syndrome. He also felt that keeping Darien involved in sports increased the likelihood that I wouldn't have problems with him running with the wrong group, trying to prove himself to be a man.

In wrestling, he would be competing against people with his own weight and would build great self-esteem, and it really did work. It was excellent advice, and Darien enjoyed wrestling, and throughout high school, I never had problems with him—never with drugs or with behavior problems. In fact, by the time he was a freshman in high school, the only problem I had with Darien was girl problems, and I was happy to have those problems, trust me! My son was a true ladies' man because we had a lot of female problems: girls calling my house at all times of the night, waking me up, trying one after another to get my son's charming voice on the phone! Those were the kinds of problems I had with him, and even though it was annoying and upsetting, I was very grateful because I knew just how special he was.

In high school, Darien never pressured me to buy him name-brand clothes; he was grateful for what I could afford. Both my sons are very frugal, and I am very thankful for that. Darien and I grew up together, and he saw me make so many mistakes in my twenties; I was so lost, and I still can't believe we survived those years. I had started smoking cigarettes; Darien hated it, and he would routinely ask me to quit. There were times when Darien would take my cigarettes and hide them from me, and when I finally decided to quit, I gave Darien my pack of cigarettes, and he would put me on an allowance of one cigarette a day until I worked my way down to a half cigarette, and it was torture. But he helped me through that tough time and we made it, and I quit smoking, thank God for that. It took me ten years to make up my mind, and I decided I loved living more than I loved cigarettes, quit cold turkey, and twenty-five years later, I never look back. Thank God for Darien always telling me he wanted me to live a long time, and that I should stop smoking.

As I watched my son grow into manhood and he neared the end of high school, I remember one night I was lying in bed, and Darien was in his senior year, and I decided it was time to have "that talk" with him, and told him that he should think about what he wanted to do with his life in terms of college, which he knew I expected him to attend. I had always emphasized education growing up in our household, so I remember telling him, "I'm going to give you a week to think about it. Then, at the end of the week, I want you to come back and tell me what you want to do with your life," and I just left him alone to think about it.

So I remember at the end of that week, I was again lying in bed, and he came in my bedroom while I was asleep, woke me up and said, "Mom, I know what it is I want to be." And when I looked at him and asked what that was, he very matter of factly replied: "I want to be a man of God, because if I'm a man of God, I know I'll be a good man."

When Darien was in his senior year, we were struggling. I couldn't afford announcements or a class ring; I could barely scrape up enough money for his cap and gown. He never complained or made me feel bad, as I promised I would get him a ring as soon as I could afford one. He never asked me to fulfill that promise, although five years later, I got him his ring. When I handed it to him, he flashed me that big smile of his that can brighten up the universe and make everyone feel good.

Darien has always been my friend, and we always talk honestly and openly with each other, and I wanted him to know I would always be there for him no matter what, and he wanted me to know the same. I tried my best to be the best mother I could be, and it has not been easy, and I'm not perfect, but I know I've been a good mother to both my boys, and no one can ever take that away from me. Like every mother, single or otherwise, raising a child who is entering that stage of crossing over into manhood, after he graduated from high school, Darien and I had a rough time. He wanted to cut the cord and do whatever he wanted to do, as all teenagers want to at age nineteen. When they finish high school, they believe they are grownups, so we fought for a while about staying out and respecting our home. Thankfully, because of the strength of our broader relationship, we worked it out and got past all the drama.

As Darien headed out into the world as a young man, he was very ambitious. He used to tell me, from the time he was a little boy, he used to say "I'm gonna make you rich, Mama, because you work so hard. Watch—one day, I'm gonna *make You rich*." And I'll admit it proudly: I *am* the kind of mother that did push my boys to excel, but I was also wise enough to stand back and let them make their own decisions. Whatever they wanted to be, I wanted them to be happy, as long as they were doing something they loved and enjoyed. I always taught them to do something that they enjoyed because they would go to work every day happy, which to me was very important.

You never, as a parent, realize how much your children really pay attention to you. I found out just how much one day when, I remember, Darien looked at me and said, "Mama, I want you to know how *much* I respect you. You don't realize how much I respect you and what I think of you. Do you know how much I respect you? Do you know that when I have my children, I want my children to be just like you?"

And I looked at him, and I said, "Son, you have paid me the highest compliment any mom could ever want.

You're telling me you want my grandkids to be like me—God, what an honor." And I never forgot that.

And as he got older, he said, "I'm going to help you..." One thing I always remember raising Darien to believe in and embrace as a child was the philosophy that giving up was never an option; it was never an option in our house; there were *no victims*. As a matter of fact, I used to tell people, "We have the two Ps: We don't want your pity, we want your prayers." We never did operate on pity, we never did feel sorry for ourselves, we just dealt with it and moved forward and kept the faith and knew that times would get better. We just kept the love in our house, kept trust in each other, and stuck together.

***

Darien: I know that's why we're still here, because of the love we have together. We're a small family, but my brother, my mother and I are so close, and we have always let that love guide us. I remember my mother always telling me, "If you have that love, you can conquer anything," and I really believe that. And that's how we live. I remember when I was in high school as a senior, and my mother was a single parent working three jobs. She worked all three of those jobs for three and a half years to provide for our family. I always looked up to my mother for what a survivor's spirit she brought to task not only in raising us, but equally in working to make sure we had a beautiful home life.

***

At the time, you needed two incomes to survive, and I didn't want to take my children just anywhere to live. So, I worked those three jobs to keep them living in a decent neighborhood; I didn't want them living in the projects because back then, drugs were really rampant in Miami with all the turf wars. With Darien in high school, I didn't want him to feel pressured because of the way the economy was, and I didn't want him to have to feel like he needed to sell drugs to help me support our family. In fact, during his senior year of high school, I gave him my car so he'd have transportation to go to work and school, so he could stay out of that kind of trouble. I rode public transportation. I was determined to make sure he didn't think he had to sell drugs to have things, and it really worked out well.

Chapter 6

Happy is the man who findeth wisdom and the man that get it understanding.

— Proverbs 3:3

RIP

Home Going of

Willie Bradford Mc Coy

March 20, 1956
to
February 24, 2005

When Darien enrolled in Miami Dade College, I remember feeling *so proud* of my son. I had always raised him to believe education was the most important asset a man could have heading out into the world, and apparently he *really* took that to heart because when he entered college, he told me he wanted, of all things, to be an educator! I remember being delighted because he was and still is great with kids—I saw that when he helped with his brother, CJ.

One particularly fond memory I have of his talent is the time when he was demonstrating to CJ the difference between walking in the dark and the light. Darien cleverly turned the light off and we were all sitting in the dark, and he asked his brother, "Can you see?" And his brother said, "No." And then after turning the light back on, Darien again asked CJ if he could see, and CJ said, "Yes." Darien did that as a demonstration of the difference between living right and living wrong: If you walk in the dark, you can't see; if you walk in the light, you can.

When Darien did that demonstration with his brother and saw how effective it was, that, he says, was when he knew he wanted to be an educator. Children just take a liking to him. And Darien never disappointed me, although I thought my dreams were shattered on that dreadful day when he fell. It seemed like he'd been robbed of everything he wanted in life. It was devastating. I spent many nights and years grieving the loss of my dreams for my son, until one day—I don't even know when it happened—I realized that Darien *is* an educator. His life has taught everyone who comes in contact with him so much, and he is still teaching us how to live and survive the worst of times. He is remarkable, and has that little extra-special something we all wish we had.

I couldn't afford to send Darien to college. He had an opportunity to go away to school, but he didn't tell me because he refused to let me take care of CJ by myself, working all the jobs I had. He feared that CJ might fall in with the wrong crowd if he didn't have the right male influence consistently around him. He wanted to be there to help me raise his brother, and so he declined to go away to college. He said to me at the time, "I'm going to get a job and pay for my own education," and he stayed home and went to Miami Dade Community College while working a full-time job.

My son was amazingly supportive. When Darien started to work, he came to me and said, "I'm going to pay you fifty dollars a week to help you out with bills," and every Saturday, without fail, he would come and put $50 on my nightstand with a rose. He never missed a week, and he never came back and asked for the money back. I still have the last rose he gave me before he had his accident; I keep it in my Bible.

To no one's surprise, Darien was very mature by the time he was in college. He went to Miami Dade and then switched schools and joined the Kappa Alpha Phi fraternity at Florida Memorial College in Miami. He was doing wonderfully—paying for his own education, working from eleven at night until seven in the morning, and he even made employee of the month. He had such an impressive work ethic and was so dedicated to paying for his schooling that he once drove in knee-high flood water to make his shift, going five miles an hour. I had begged him not to go. That, to me, was a reflection of how very committed he was to getting his degree.

Darien, Commencement Ceremony

Part II
The Accident

Chapter 7

For he shall give his angels charge over thee, to keep thee in all thy ways.

—Psalms 91:11

Darien, six years old

Following 7-11, Darien got a job with a Miami branch of a national hardware/home-improvement retail chain. In hindsight, I can't tell you the times I cried and regretted Darien's working for this company. I had been working there two years prior to Darien, and he'd been hired on after he'd graduated from high school.

Everyone liked Darien, and I used to hear good things about him from his friends who worked with him. I was proud but wanted more for him, and kept pushing him to stay in college. I remember that approximately one month before his accident, he started catching the bus to school, and when I enquired as to why, he told me he enjoyed taking the bus and walking. It's amazing how things turned out. I'm so glad he had those walks, and can still see him now walking home, and can still see him dancing—I will always see him that way.

Darien and I would go every morning before work to a nature trail near our home. I would walk and he would jog. He was in excellent shape at the time of his accident. Darien was a positive example for his friends and coworkers—even the older workers looked up to him. He is a natural-born leader, and even now he radiates strength, confidence, faith and love.

Before he got hurt, Darien never missed a day of work, and he worked at this company for almost two years through rain or shine; he'd roll through a flood to get to work.

***

Darien: At the time, I was working in the cabinet section of the store. One day was like the next until the day that changed my life forever. I remember I was on a lift, putting some boxes up on a shelf; my supervisor had ordered me to get the boxes up and didn't care how I did it. He was expecting the company's field supervisor to come in and do an inspection of the store, and it was my boss' goal to have the whole warehouse cleaned up prior to his arrival—even if, as it turned out, it quite literally meant breaking our necks to get it done.

I remember feeling that it wasn't safe because there wasn't really enough room on the shelf I was trying to stock, and unfortunately I was right. When I got up there to put the boxes on the shelf, the inventory was so high, I had to take off my safety belt to reach it; lift I was standing on wouldn't go that high. When I did that, all of a sudden the beam from the shelf popped out and knocked me off the lift, and I fell twenty feet. Along the way, I hit my head on the wall so hard that, I later learned, I knocked a big hole in the wall with the back of my head. I remember landing on my butt in a daze.

***

After Darien fell, they told him to go to the break room to rest his head and take a nap. That was their answer. He began complaining about his head hurting after that. I'll never forget getting a phone call at home in the middle of the night, telling me that my son had fallen and that they were on the way home with him. The first thing I asked his supervisor was, "If he fell, why aren't you sending him to the emergency room?"

When he got home, he was out of it, and his buddies from work who had brought him took him straight to his bedroom. I remember asking Darien directly why he hadn't gone to the doctor, but I could see he was kind of out of it so I let him rest. It wasn't until the next day that I got his supervisor on the phone and asked again, "Why didn't you take him to the doctor and let him get checked out?"

He kept telling me that Darien had said he was alright, and I kept reminding them that because he'd been hurt on their property, they were responsible and should have sent him to the doctor. I was arguing back and forth with the supervisor; Darien was nineteen years old, he said he was fine, but he didn't understand like I understood. He could have had internal injuries. After the third day of going back and forth, the supervisor stopped taking my calls.

Darien was home, laid up in bed, for about a week. After that, he said he was feeling better and wanted to go back to work. I had a horrible feeling in my stomach over it, and my anxiety was so bad, I was begging him not to go back to work. He was a man, though, and said he had to because of school and son on. So, he returned to work.

I remember being especially worried because of his telling me before he left that he had this funny feeling in the back of his neck. I said, "You need to go see the doctor!" But he went back to work instead, and I kept calling the store to complain. "You need to get my child checked out, he needs to get X-rays," I told them, but to no avail.

A week later, Darien was in the same warehouse, moving some boxes around, and the pallet jack he was using broke and hit him in the head. After my son had suffered yet another head injury, what did the crackpot management team do in response? The *same thing*: They sent him home to me!

***

Darien: By this time, my mother was not just kind of pissed off, but *real* pissed off that I'd gotten hurt twice on this job. This claimed to be a big, family-oriented company, and still she went back and forth with them for about a month while I kept going back to work. I was getting so razzed by my co-workers that finally, I said to my mother, "Mom, don't call my job anymore because they're giving me a hard time, calling me a mama's boy and saying that all you want is a lawsuit." I explained that I didn't want to lose my job, and so asked her to back off. I promised to let her know if I got in a lot of pain.

***

What could I say? My son had clearly said, "Back off. I don't want to lose my job. They're harassing me about it." So, not wanting to cause him to lose his job, I backed up—a move I would regret for years afterwards.

Granddaddy Willie D McCoy, R.I.P.

Chapter 8

And when the Lord saw her, he had compassion on her, and said unto her, "Weep not."

—Luke 7:13

Linda, Auntie Dee, Auntie Freida and Grandma (seated), 1994

Two or three months down the road, I was at home, getting ready for bed, and around midnight—the same time the call about Darien's first accident had come—my phone rang. It was again Darien's manager, only this time, instead of telling me not worry about it, he told me they'd had to rush Darien to the emergency room. Apparently, Darien had been complaining about sharp pains shooting from his neck to his head, bad enough to scare his co-workers into rushing him to get medical care.

So, I called my mother up and we immediately headed to Palmetto Hospital. When we got there, nobody told me how serious it really was. All I was thinking at that point was, *He's finally going to get some X-rays, and they're going to give him something for his head pain.* Once I went up to his room, however, I found Darien lying in bed with all these tubes stuck in him, and he was unresponsive to me.

I panicked and ran out of the room in the hospital, and eventually found myself sitting on a bench in front of the building in a state of shock. I couldn't believe that I had just seen my son like that, and I just started praying. I remembered everything I'd been taught when I was a little girl about prayer and my faith. Once I'd gotten my strength back, I went back into the hospital, found my mother and said, "Let's go back into Darien's room and pray for him," and we did just that.

I put my hands on his and said to him, "You can't die. You cannot die. You have to come back because your brother needs you." When I said that, a tear came down from his eye, and he opened his eye. The doctor ran in and said they'd been working on him for a long time and he hadn't been responsive to them; they were amazed at the fact that he had responded to me.

When Darien came to, I was talking to him but he couldn't talk back to me. He just kept looking around and couldn't move his lips. I kept asking what was wrong with him, and the doctors kept replying that no one could figure out what the problem was. But after running more tests, the doctor took me aside and explained, out of Darien's earshot, that he couldn't move because he was paralyzed from the mouth down. He couldn't breathe on his own, either, and they had to put him on a respirator. He also couldn't talk.

I said, "He can't talk?" Of course, I felt an instant nervousness come over me. I just couldn't believe it. The whole reality of it was just beyond belief to me—that my child was laying there and all he could do was move his eyeballs around, and he couldn't communicate with me.

The doctors moved Darien to intensive care, and there he stayed there for about three weeks while the hospital was busy trying to figure out what was wrong with him.

My sister, Frieda, and her children were among the first to arrive; they had driven all night to be there for Darien. We slept on the hard floor for days, praying and waiting for an answer. We all knew it was critical. As bad as Darien's situation was, and though we weren't encouraged by medical prognosis, we did find comfort in the fact that day after day, the waiting room was so full—wall to wall—with so many people I didn't know but who knew my son. They stayed for days, praying with us for Darien, and there was so much love in that waiting room that one day, a nurse came to me and asked who Darien was. She thought he was a celebrity because she'd never seen so many people in the waiting room praying for one patient. She told me, "He must be a very special young man," to which I replied, "Yes he is, he's very special."

I remember walking the halls of the hospital, praying the twenty-third psalm over and over again, saying to myself and God, "I know he will not die." I can't explain the emotions I felt inside; it was as if I was in another zone where I felt safe, and where the answers would come to me if I just stayed there and sought direction. It seemed like an eternity passed and no one had any answers, so I just kept praying.

I could hardly walk; my legs felt like noodles, my heart was broken, and our lives had been turned upside down and inside out. My mother would not leave me, even when I went to the restroom—she would stand at the door when I came out. When I fell on my knees, she fell on her knees; I must have done this at least ten times a day. I just couldn't stay off my knees, begging and praying for mercy for my son. It was desperate prayer, with no boundaries. I wanted the angels in heaven to hear me, and to reach God Himself, so I wasn't ashamed to show my emotions out loud. I didn't care. I needed supernatural help.

Friends from work: Powell, Mark, Todd and Derrick with Darien, 1994

Chapter 9

Now faith is the substance of things hopeful, the evidence of things not seen.

—Hebrews 11:1

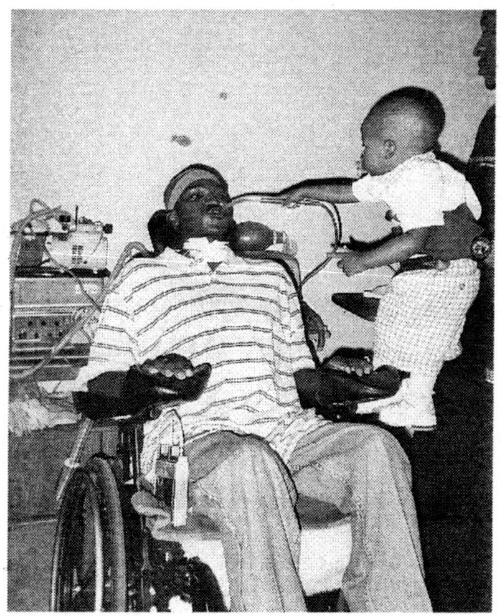

CJII (one year old) suctioning Uncle D

Finally, the hospital staff realized that Darien's condition was too much for them to handle, so they airlifted him over to Jackson Memorial Hospital. When he arrived, two neurosurgeons, Dr. Bart Green and Dr. David Noble, both examined him.

When I arrived, they told me that Darien's injury was more severe than any they had ever seen.

As they explained it, the specific injury had caused an infarct on his brain stem, and no one had ever lived with an injury level that high. (Little did I know that would soon become a theme for us: Darien outliving all the doctors' odds—and everyone else's too.) To underscore the latter, his doctors told me that medical science could not help Darien, and that if he had gotten to them at the onset of the injury, they could have stopped it and saved him. Sadly, as I had feared from the start, because his superiors at work had waited three months to send him to a doctor, the damage had been done and there was nothing anybody could do at that point.

Dr. Noble said that Darien was the twenty-fifth person in medical history to have an injury like that, and that with the other twenty-four people, what had happened to them had only become apparent during their autopsies. He told me that Darien's prognosis at that time was death; he said to me, "Your son is not going to live." And I remember I looked at the doctor, dumbfounded, and asked, "What do you mean?" He continued, "He's not going to live. No one has ever lived with an injury this high."

After that, all I could do was go back to Darien's room to see how he felt about that. I expected he would be up for the fight I knew was coming.

The hospital staff had given me a little chart with the alphabet on it to communicate with Darien, and I put it in front of him and asked him to tell me what he wanted me to do. As I pointed to each letter, he would blink if it was the letter he wanted, and I wrote out what he spelled: I WANT TO LIVE. Then, he spelled I WILL WALK AGAIN. And I told him, "If want to live, you can live. If you believe that you will walk again, if your faith is out there where you believe you will walk again, I'm going to step out there and put my faith right there with you. I got your back! I'm right by your side. If you say it, I'm going to stand by you and never leave you, no matter what, I promise."

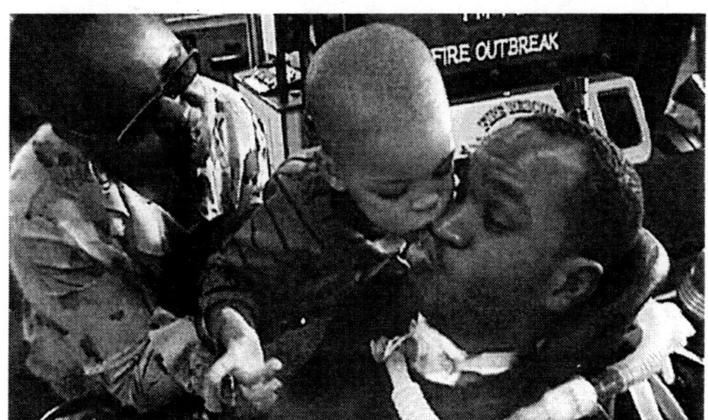

CJII's second Birthday party

Chapter 10

There was a man in the land of Uz, whose name was Job; and that man was perfect and upright, and one that feared God and eschewed evil.

—Job 1:1

Linda and CJI, 2008

On the second day of knowing the reality of Darien's prognosis, he was very upset and asked me the question, 'Why did God allow this to happen to me? He knows how much I love Him. Why would He allow this to happen to me?"

At the time, I didn't have an answer for him; I couldn't tell him why, which frustrated me almost over and above anything else. I went home to my mother's house and kneeled down in prayer and searched for answers, and said to God: "I taught my son everything you told me—to love you, to be a good man, everything—and he's asking me why, and I don't have an answer for why this happened."

Then, the spirit said to me, "Go tell him to remember Job."

So I went back to the hospital and said to Darien, "Remember Job. He was a good man. Job didn't do anything wrong, but his faith was tested, and God allowed these things to happen to him to test his faith and see if he would believe in Him no matter what. Job kept the faith, and God honored that and restored to Job everything that had been taken away from him.

"Job hadn't done anything particularly wrong to cause these things to happen to him. You didn't do anything wrong, either. This is just a test. You're going to have to believe God. If you believe you're going to walk again, you're going to have to believe that God will make it happen."

I could see that Darien believed in what I was telling him. I can't lie and say that a serenity came over us in that moment, but I believe that we both felt that we had a little better handle on the reins of the journey before us, which I knew would be fundamental to our survival in the days—let alone years—to come.

Darien was in college when he had the accident. In its tragic aftermath, as word got around to everyone who had grown up with him, all his cousins and friends came to me, asking as a chorus the same universal question we've all asked since day one: Why Darien? His friends would go on to say, as part of that question that he was the good one, the one who, when they went to the clubs, wouldn't drink, and used to tell everyone not to do drugs, not to drink, and to get on the right path.

From a young age, it was Darien's mission to help people who were on drugs get off them, having had the example of his father, a drug user who lost his life over it in 1991. Ironically, Darien's father died of a head injury, and two years later, Darien had his own in the accident, which to this day blows my mind when I think about it.

I remember, throughout those earliest days following his accident, telling God, "I can't believe you're going to take my son away. I just don't believe that you'd to that to me." And he's proven himself very faithful and is still here today, so I'm grateful for that.

Darien stayed at the hospital in Miami, Florida, for about a month, after which the staff said to me that they couldn't keep him there any longer because they didn't have any facilities to help a patient like Darien, with a level of injury as high as his. Because he had defied the odds and hadn't died as all the experts had predicted, they finally said, "Well, he's not dead, so we have to send him somewhere." So, they gave me three choices: Shepherd Spinal Center in either Atlanta, New Jersey or California.

As fate would have it, my sister was working as a respiratory therapist with paralyzed people at Shepherd's Spinal Center in Atlanta. So, she went to the staff and explained what had happened to her nephew, and arrangements were made for Darien to be flown by air ambulance all the way from Miami to Atlanta. When Darien was leaving on the trip, as they rolled out of the ICU and to the ambulance, my sister was bagging him, giving him breath, and she looked at his face, and he looked up at her and said, "I love you," and she said, "I love you too, baby," and that was the last thing I heard him say. When we left Miami forever.

***

Darien's aunt/head homecare nurse: I'm the one who transported him to Shepherd's Spinal Center. I worked there as a respiratory therapist, so I went to my administrators there to get Darien admitted because he did not have a rehab center in Miami. When you work in that field, you know that even if a person is paralyzed, he's still able to be rehabilitated in certain areas so that he can live a quality life. You want to get those patients to that way of living, and I knew that. I went with the transport team to pick Darien up from Miami and transported him up to Shepherd's in Atlanta, and he was more critical than some of the patients there because of his respiratory status.

Darien, fifteen years old, Linda and Cameron

Part III
The Aftermath

Chapter 11

But my God shall supply all your needs according to His riches and glory, by Christ Jesus.

—Philippians 4:19

Dr. Osborne-(internal medicine), Shawn, Auntie Dee and Darien

When we arrived in Atlanta, we had to get on welfare because I had to quit my job, leave everything and go there and get help for Darien. Without question, once that happened to Darien, he became my number-one priority, and all I thought about was him because his life was on the line.

I never regretted my decision to help my son, though there were times when I was very, very lonely and very much afraid and didn't know what to do. What I did know was that my focus had to become taking care of Darien, keeping the family together and making sure that his brother, CJ, had some kind of normalcy in his life. So, I just focused in on taking care of them and took myself totally out of the equation.

I had to leave everything—my house, my car—throw some things in a suitcase and go right behind Darien, the next day, from Miami to Atlanta. When I got to Shepherd's, Darien's new doctor, Dr. Leslie, said to me, "You know Darien's situation is grave. He's the worst patient to ever come into our center. We don't know how to care for him. Nobody knows what to do for Darien, because he is a first. We have never had anybody this bad before, so there is no protocol for him. So, you do understand the situation is grave?"

I said, "I've been told that, but Darien says he wants to live, so I believe him. If he says he wants to live, then I will stand by him, and he's going to live."

They admitted him there and set up a program as best they could.

I had thought those years were over—taking care of Darien—and it broke my heart when I thought of the places he could have gone and things he could have done if this had not happened to him. When this first happened and the doctors told me that he would never have children, I went to bed that night and had a dream about Darien's father. He was just standing there; he never said a word, just looked at me, and he was smiling, with an expression of admiration on his face. He was so happy. And I remember asking him in the dream, "Can you see what's going on with Darien, what's happening to him?" He never answered me.

In the room I was in during the dream, there were three little children and two bunk beds. I was n the bottom bed and one of the three kids was on top; the other two were in a second set of bunk beds across from me. I was looking at them and couldn't figure out who they were.

The next day, as I walked down the hall of a rehab hospital with Darien, I asked him, "Have you ever thought about having children?"

And he said, "Yeah."

I said, "How many kids do you want to have?"

"I always wanted three kids," he said.

"Darien," I replied, "I saw your three children last night: two boys and a girl, and that little girl? Thou shall name her Linda." To this day, this remains our in joke; every now and then, I'll get in his face and remind him that he owes me three grandchildren.

Chapter 12

I can do all things through Christ which strengthens me.

—Philippians 4:13

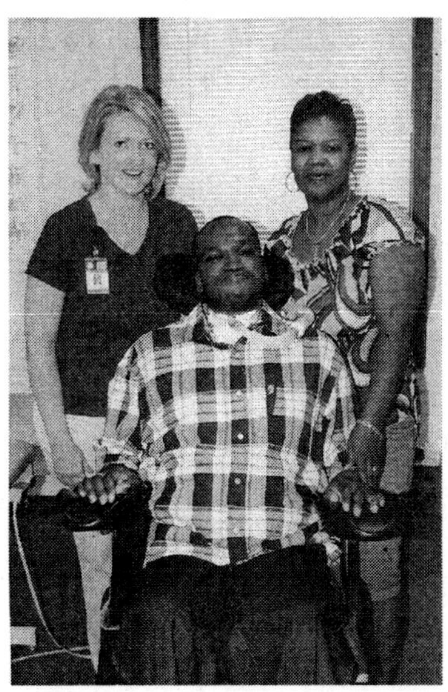

Marie-(speech therapist), Darien and Carolyn-(respratory therapist)

Darien was at Shepherd's for eight months, and that entire time, he coded three or four times a day. That meant that he was dying, and the nurses had to do CPR to resuscitate him. His resolve to live was really a challenge. Every time he coded, they had to call for respiratory to come and bring him back, and I stayed in there with him; I wouldn't leave his side. When he was about to code, he could feel it coming; he would choke and lose air, and he would tell me what was going on. Because I was in the room with him and was seeing him do it so much, I knew what to do to kind of help him till the team got to him.

Whenever he felt like he was coding, he would let me know. He would say, "Get the bag, get the oxygen." And then we had this thing we always said to each other: "F.E.A.R. What is fear? FALSE EVIDENCE APPEARING TO BE REAL." Every time Darien would code, we would look at each other and say "F.E.A.R.," and I would bag him and work with him till the team got there. Then, they would take over, and he would come around. I did this for eight months with him.

***

> Darien's aunt/head homecare nurse: The level of Darien's injury caused his phrenic nerve to not function—the nerve that enables you to breathe and stimulates your diaphragm. Because of the level of the injury, his phrenic nerve was not able to innovate the diaphragm for breathing. So, his breathing arrested because the diaphragm was no longer working, because the phrenic nerve was not doing what it needed to do and Darien could not breath on his own.

When that infarct hit the stem of Darien's brain, it caused him to lose his breathing and the ability to move his body all at once—so he was a quadriplegic, ventilator-dependant patient. His respiratory function was one of the biggest problems, though, along with his inability to maintain a sitting position. Even when we brought him home after a whole year at Shepherd's, Darien still suffered in those areas. It took him a while to adjust to sitting up real straight; he'd always have to sit in a semi-like position because he could not adjust to the blood flow.

Once Darien was at Shepherd's, in the early days, Linda wouldn't leave his side. When you're on a ventilator, it's hooked to an alarm, and whenever he went into a problem, the alarm would go off and we'd have to rush to the room to help Darien. When he was first admitted, he was admitted into the intensive care unit, and at the beginning of his injury, he was very fragile because he was having plugging problems. If he got a mucus plug he wasn't getting any air and he could have gone into respiratory arrest. Also, Darien was having violent seizure-like activities—not seizures, but muscle spasms that were so bad he'd shake the bed as if he were having a seizure. Then, when we set him up in a chair, he was very fragile because of his blood flow; quadriplegics are not able to manage a change in position, so when they sit up, they might faint.

Darien was very fragile in all of those areas when he first came in, and so we had to work through all of that to find out what was going on and what we could do to help him. Linda was there and saw all of that going on; obviously, she wasn't going to leave her child. She wanted to be there just in case the nurses didn't hear the alarm. Darien was very fragile for the first three or four months at Shepherd's.

***

When it got to the fifth month of them having to bring him back so much, they had a meeting with all the doctors and administrators and even the chaplain, who called me down to his office and said, "We had a meeting and decided that we want you to sign a DNR—a 'do not resuscitate' order."

I said, "No, I'm not going to do that."

So then, the chaplain said to me, "Nobody should have to live like this. If you don't go in and tell Darien, I will."

And I looked at him and said, "You are supposed to be a man of faith. My son is in his right mind. He's not a vegetable, and he says he wants to live. Every time he codes, I want you to bring him back. Now, if you go in my son's room and discourage him and speak about death to him, I promise you I will kick your ASS all over this hospital."

God forgive me, but that was what I said I'd do to him if he spoke about death to my son.

It was clear that at least he had gotten my point, because the next day, when I went into Darien's room, the chaplain came to visit, and he had all kinds of spiritual readings for Darien. He also brought us VCR tapes of Charles Stanley, who is a well-known minister at the First Baptist Church in Georgia and a very good teacher. Darien and I played those tapes all day long and listened to music, and afterward, I went down to the chaplain's office and thanked him. I said, "Now we're on the same page."

Darien and I kept listening to those tapes, and he kept coding, but we persevered and kept praying, and had other people at the hospital who prayed with us.

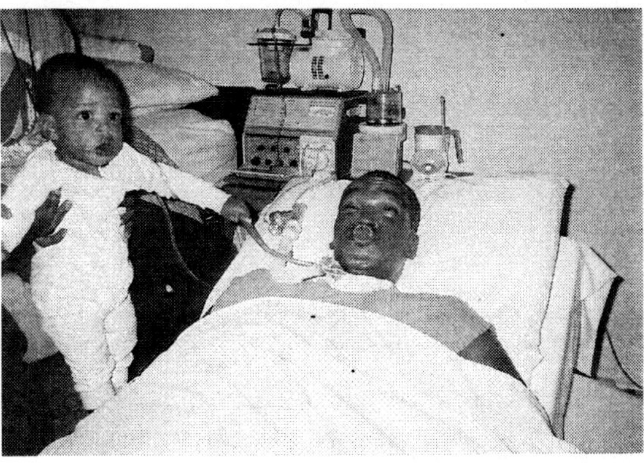

CJII (nine months old) suctioning Uncle D mouth

Chapter 13

> My breath is corrupt, my days are extinct, the graves are ready for me.
>
> —Job 17:1

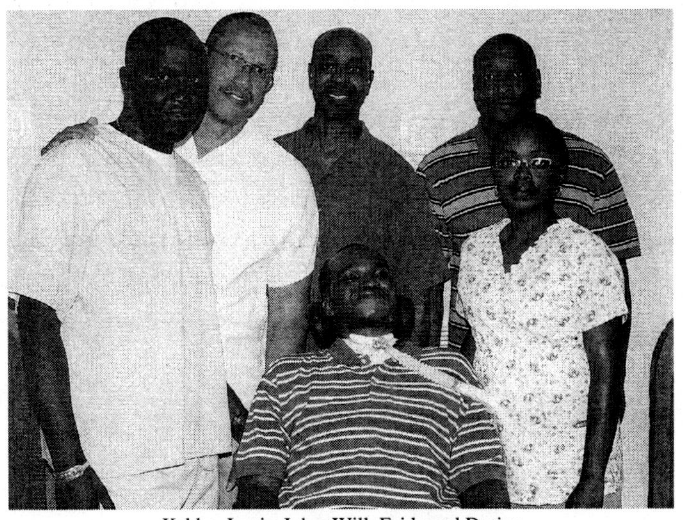

Kebba, Jarvis, John, Will, Feida and Darien

In the meantime, Darien had lost weight, getting down to eighty pounds from 155! It got so bad that his tailbone actually poked through his skin at one point—that's how skinny he was. So, they were trying to work on that sore to get that well.

His specialist, Dr. Leslie, would come to me every

Friday before he went home and say, "You know Darien's situation is grave. Do you know how serious this is?" And every Friday, I'd look him in his eyes and say, "We'll see you on Monday morning." And sure enough, Monday morning when he'd come back, Darien would still be alive.

Finally, they got tired of how much money it was costing to keep Darien alive and give him CPR, and so they sent me to the psychiatrist. She said, "You know, everybody thinks there's something wrong with you."

I patiently listened to her and then replied, "I want you to know that I see what you see. I see him sitting in that wheelchair and see death warmed over him. I see what you see. But I don't believe it. It's not so. He's not going to die. Darien says he wants to live. I'm not on a natural level, I'm on a spiritual level here, and I'm not coming down for you or anybody else."

I felt that I had *no choice*—I had to stay on a spiritual level because if I took my eyes off of God for one split second, I know I would lose it. Darien said that both of us had to stay on a spiritual level. So, I told the psychiatrist, "I'm not coming down. I'm gonna stay here. I'm not coming down. Every time he codes, they'd better bring him back." And I refused to leave his bedside because of the politics involved—and believe me when I say there were *definitely* politics at play.

When we'd gotten to Atlanta, we'd discovered that the president of the company Darien had worked for when he'd had his accident was chairman of the board at Shepherd. That turned out to be the source of all of the talk about Darien's treatment being too much money and the staff's chorus of, "You need to let him go on."

I said, "No. *Nobody* has the right to take his life. You're going to keep him alive.' And knowing the politics at play, I wouldn't leave him: I slept in his room the entire eight months that he was at Shepherd's, with the exception of maybe three weeks when someone came and relieved me. I wouldn't leave his side because I was afraid that if he coded, no one would come to resuscitate him.

As the months wore on and on, I often went down to the chapel and prayed so hard and so loud that I didn't realize I was screaming and begging God not to take Darien's life. "Please, bring him back!" I was apparently praying so forcefully that they could hear me up on the second floor, where Darien was staying. At one point a nurse came down to the chapel and said, "Linda, you're gonna make yourself sick. We can hear you on the second floor. You can't keep going like this." Still, I wouldn't listen to her, and just screamed and prayed and begged God not to take Darien's life.

Then, all of a sudden, Darien gained two pounds! Then two more pounds! Then his weight started coming back on, and after eight months, they discharged him from Shepherd's. They wanted to put him in a nursing home, which I was adamantly against. They knew that if he went to a nursing home, he wouldn't last.

At that time, I didn't have anywhere to take him when he was discharged, as I was living at my sister's. So, I got on the phone, but I couldn't get an attorney because his situation was handled by worker's compensation, and because every lawyer I called talked to the doctor and he told them that Darien wasn't going to live. Based on that, they refused to represent him.

So, on top of being there to bring Darien back, I had to be his attorney and talk to the insurance company. I kept insisting to them, "Look, they're going to discharge him. We need a place to stay." And the adjuster would say, "You keep calling us, bugging us about a house, and the doctor says Darien is not going to live. You sound like a crazy lady."

"Well, you're not God," I would reply. "Darien ain't dead yet, and when he's discharged, we need some place to stay."

"Well, we'll put him in a nursing home,' the insurance adjuster would say.

I would respond, "That will never happen. If you put him in a nursing home, you'd better put him in a room big enough for me and his brother, because you will not separate my family. You're not going to separate us. Wherever Darien goes, his brother and I go with him."

Part IV
Going Home

Chapter 14

Preserve me, oh God, for in thee do I put my trust.
—Psalms 16:1

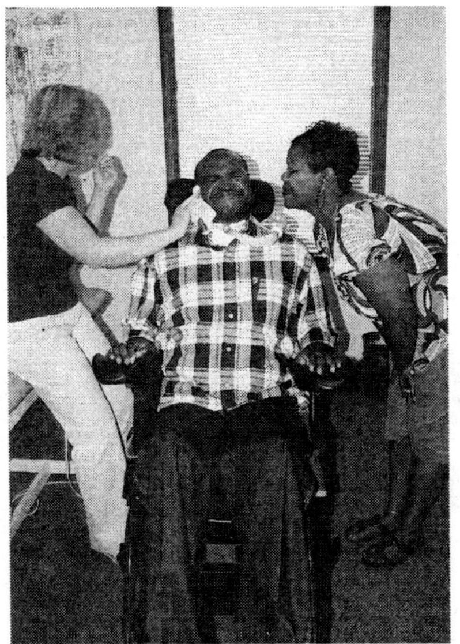

Marie-(speech therapist), Darien
and Carolyn-(respratory therapist) sharing a laugh

Finally, I talked to my nephew, who opened up his house and said we could stay there until I found housing for us. Not surprisingly, when Shepherd's discharged Darien, they didn't give me any referrals to any doctors; those who worked at Shepherd's refused to work with Darien. The politics of it all was at work against us yet again. They just sent Darien out the front door to die.

I said to my sister, who worked there as a respiratory therapist, "I need you to come home with me and help me with Darien." So, she went to her supervisors and told them that she was leaving, and they said, "He's not going to live past two weeks. You sure you want to resign from your job? Two weeks tops—he'll be gone." To this day, I'm so grateful and proud that she replied, "I don't care if he lives two weeks. My sister needs me and I'm gonna go home and help her." She resigned from her job and came home with me, and we went and stayed in my nephew's dining area.

***

Darien's aunt/head homecare nurse: Before you come home from a rehab center, nurses have to be trained to take care of you, as does your family. As a patient, you have to be trained to instruct someone how to take care of you. As a caregiver, though you might already have the equipment you need, when you're setting a patient up at home, you have to fit him into a quality lifestyle and not act like he's sick.

First, Darien came home for three days and we were provided with a nursing agency that wasn't working. We had to call 911 twice; the second time the EMTs told Linda that they needed to take

Darien back to the hospital. They were afraid to do certain things that had to be done with patients like Darien, to clear the mucus out of the lungs—we call it "quad coughing." This was to assist Darien in coughing up the stuff he couldn't cough up himself. But they were afraid because of his frailty.

I didn't come home with Darien until he arrested that second time, after he'd been sent to the hospital. He'd told his mother, "I'm not going home again with those nurses." That was when I quit my job at Shepherd's and came home full time to help take care of Darien. I felt that God had already trained me to take care of Darien both in respiratory care and as a nurse—I was trained to do both. It also was reassuring for Darien that I was there with him once he'd returned home.

***

I remember when I brought Darien home from the hospital. He had tubes everywhere; they even fed him through his nose. He seemed so helpless and frail, like death was right there to take him away from us. I prayed so hard, and God gave me the wisdom to take the tube out of Darien's nose. I couldn't stand to see him like that, and I could tell that he didn't like it either. When I had his permission to remove the tube, I went to the pharmacy and found a formula that I thought had enough calories in it for him. When my sister took the tube out of his nose, we started feeding him from the tube in his stomach. My sister reassured me that he could survive on formula alone and get all the nutrients he needed.

Not surprisingly, when the health insurance company finally sent a nursing agency to take care of Darien, the nurses had no experience with his type of injury. Prior to that, I had done some research and found a nursing agency that had more experience taking care of patients like Darien who were ventilator-dependent. I had asked the insurance company to give me that agency, and instead they'd sent somebody out there who wasn't qualified to do the job.

To temporarily remedy the situation, the insurance company ended up paying me $12 an hour to assist the nurses in taking care of Darien. I called the director of the nursing agency that the insurance company had forced us to use and said, "If anything should happen to Darien because your nurses aren't qualified to do CPR on him, I'm going to come at you with both barrels open!" At that point, the nursing agency dropped Darien as a patient.

When they had first sent this agency out, Darien had coded, and the nurses hadn't known how to do CPR, so my nephew and I had jumped in and did it and brought Darien back. My nephew had to go to work, and I was left there with Darien alone, and he coded on me again; I started bagging him and the nurse called 911. When the EMTs got there, one of them told me, "You know what, ma'am? We don't know how to do CPR on your son. We've never dealt with anybody like this." We were able to get Darien to come around. The chief of the fire station asked me if I would come in and teach his men how to do CPR on somebody like Darien so that if I called on them again, his men would know what to do for him.

Eventually, God sent angels from everywhere. Nurses came and helped us take care of Darien, including Carolyn, a.k.a. "night nurse" or "Aunt Carol." She has been with Darien for sixteen years. Like my sister, she left the hospital to come and help set up a care program for Darien, and they are both so faithful to him.

***

> Nurse Carolyn: I first met Darien at Shepherd's Spinal Center, when he was admitted. I was a nurse tech at that time. When I saw him come in, my heart went out to him because he was a very sick young man. I was impressed with the fact that his family was so supportive of him—his mom and his aunt were there twenty-four/seven. When Darien got ready to go home was when I first got to meet Linda. Another RN who was going to be part of the homecare team couldn't take the job because it was a weekend shift, and she went to church on Sundays. So, I took the position because weekends worked perfectly for me.

I started out working nights with him then, and of course he was asleep at night. We were still trying to get him well. The main concerns on the medical side were trying to maintain the suctioning of his secretions, because he had copious amounts of them. We would have to suction him quite a bit; we could hear it when he was having secretions, and his ventilator would go off if he needed suctioning. It would make a sound to let us know if just in case we didn't hear Darien suctioning, but most times we could hear him. Once we were alerted to his secreting, we had to take care of it immediately because there was so much of it. Now the secretions aren't as bad as they were at first, but back then it was immediate.

Another concern was turning him frequently to prevent blood clotting and bed sores. If he lay on one side too long, he could get irritations on his skin, like on the ankles and knees, which would cause redness that could eventually develop into a sore. He had to be turned every hour starting out, and then we worked our way up to three hours, depending on how he tolerated each hour. We had to make sure he didn't develop any bed sores and make sure there weren't any open areas. A bed sore is very serious because of the potential for infection, so we made sure that his skin was never exposed. He has never had a bed sore in the sixteen years we've been working with him.

Darien can wear a T-shirt at night, but he doesn't

wear anything else when he sleeps. He's covered up, but we have to make sure to pad him with a pillow between his legs and up under his knees. When he's turned onto his side, a pillow goes under his back to take the pressure off it. Turning him every two to three hours relieves the pressure from his back, shoulders, knees and ankles, where he can get red areas very quickly.

He has a special mattress also, which helps prevent bed sores. It can actually turn him if we put it on that mode, but we prefer to turn him ourselves because we can make sure he gets a good turn. But that's the best type of mattress to have for a patient with a condition like Darien's, who's going to be in the bed for a long period of time.

***

Darien's aunt/head homecare nurse: Day to day, I stay focused on Darien's care and on administering prophylactic care. I have to do whatever I can to keep him from getting bed sores, so at night, he gets turned every three hours. During the day, his skin cannot rest against railings and he cannot wear certain clothes; for example, he can't sit in jeans all day. We have to stay focused on anything that can cause him to have a pressure sore.

Anytime we see an area where there is a little rash or a scratch from a nurse's fingernail—hey, things happen—we can't just look at it and go, "Oh, he got a scratch" and dismiss it. We have to say, "Oh, my God, he's going to get a pressure sore there" and work with it to make sure it doesn't become a sore or anything else he's subject to getting.

If Darien gets a bedsore, he can get an infection because there's no circulation, and you need good circulation for something like that to heal well. If you don't have good circulation, that won't happen. So you have to work with it at the beginning so it doesn't get to that point.

I had to train the nurses respiratory-wise, because nurses are not taught strictly in respiratory; they're not taught how to operate the vents and whatnot because in a hospital, they have a respiratory department to operate that equipment for them. That was the most challenging part—training the home nurses in respiratory. I laid out Darien's care-plan for them and got them acclimated to his care, focusing on his skin and working prophylactically to keep him from getting pneumonia. His bed sheets had to be smooth so he wouldn't get bed sores, and we had to rotate him in the bed so that he wasn't laying on bulky areas where the sheets were all balled up or with his leg and arm all twisted up against the rail—anything that would cause pressure on the skin.

Also, Linda and I had to train the nurses in the

bagging process, which occurs when there is a thick secretion and sometimes when we get him up in a chair. If he sits straight up, the blood will rush straight down to the lower part of his body. If he gets like that, he's going to pass out, and when he passes out, you get a bag and give him some breaths to bring him back up. It's just like if you faint and someone slaps you in the face to get you conscious again.

When we bag him, what we're doing is breathing for him rapidly, giving him fast breaths; the vent gives Darien twelve breaths a minute and with the bag, we're trying to give him twenty if we can. We give him rapid, good breaths to bring him back through, and then if the suction is the reason why he passed out, if he had a plug, we suction him out. If it was his blood flow, we recline him for a while and allow his body to get leveled so the flow of blood is level again.

***

Nurse Carolyn: If Darien codes, it takes one person to bag him and another to suction him. We give him whatever it takes per minute along the lines of normal CPR—two breaths, et cetera—but over his trachea instead of his mouth.

Chapter 15

Plead my cause oh Lord with them who strive with me; fight against them that fight against me.

—Psalms 35:1

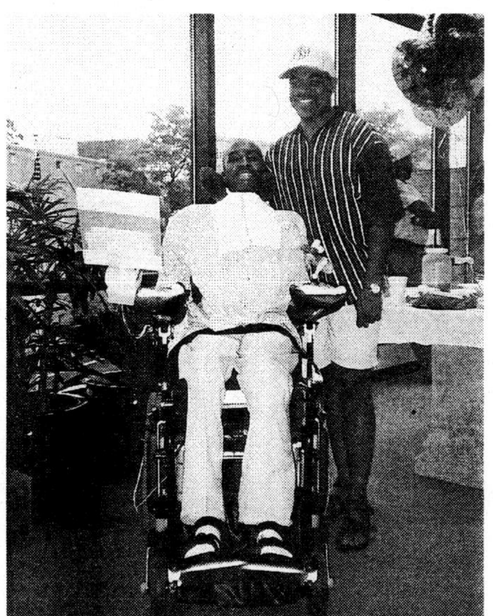

Darien and Cousin Cameron Dixon

After my initial dealings with both the hospital and the insurance company, it became clear to me that I would need to hire legal assistance to settle all of the issues—medical, legal or otherwise—that kept popping up in our path toward Darien's recovery. I'd initially retained council to handle the mediation with the insurance and third-party carriers, but we had to get rid of that first attorney because he was crooked. He tried to sell us out and force me into an early settlement. After he presented the offer to us, I told him firmly, "No!" He said, "This is a lot of money." And I replied, "Well, it may be a lot of money, but I've never done this before, and I don't know if it's enough money to take care of Darien."

I went home, prayed about it and then went to First Union and Bank of America and Prudential Insurance. I told them how much it took to take care of Darien on a monthly basis including his nurses, supplies and so on, and asked them to give me a breakdown of how much it would cost to keep Darien alive for the next forty years. They did the numbers; the figure was so high, and so much more than what the attorney had wanted me to settle for. I went back to him and rejected the offer.

He said, "But this is a lot of money."

I said, "I don't care. This money isn't for me. It's to keep Darien alive."

He was acting like the money was for me. It wasn't enough money, and he kept trying to push the settlement issue so I fired him, and we hired the lawyer who is still with us—Jerry Goodmark.

***

Jerry Goodmark: I've specialized in worker's compensation for forty years. I passed the bar in 1969, and my dad had specialized in worker's comp since 1935, so that's basically what our firm does.

When I began working on Linda and Darien's case, as I recall, an attorney was handling it and they didn't want him any longer. Then, another attorney, who is also a mediator, took the case on but did not feel that he could handle his mediation practice as well this case due to its magnitude. He knew that I specialized in catastrophic injuries and recommended us to Linda and Darien.

My first meeting with Linda McCoy left me with the opinion that this case ranked at the very top of the catastrophic-injury list. Being a ventilated quadriplegic is as disabled as you can get. Darien's initial specialist, Dr. Leslie, who was the head of Shepherd's Spinal Center in Atlanta, told us when we took his deposition on December 5, 2002 that Darien was the longest-living ventilator quadriplegic they had ever had at Shepherd's—and they have probably more patients like that than any other place in the country. Darien has lived seven more years since that deposition, which is just incredible. I'd heard of such things, but had never seen anyone who was as catastrophically injured as Darien.

Chapter 16

Then sayeth the Lord unto me, thou hast well seen,
for I will hasten my word to perform it.
—Jeremiah 1:12

Linda and grandson CJII, 2008

Darien stayed in my nephew's house as the months wore on, and I kept fighting with the insurance company and asking them for housing. One thing the case manager told me was that because Darien's father was deceased, Darien was entitled to some Social Security benefits from him.

So, in addition to contacting attorneys we had to get Darien's name changed on his birth certificate so he could apply for those benefits.

I finally found one worker's comp attorney who, after hearing my case, said of the insurance company, "Well, they're not God, they can't say how long he's gonna live." When he took the case, he started fighting for housing, and we had so many emergency hearings before the judge in order to get housing for Darien. Finally, the insurance company said to me, "Here are your options: He either goes into a nursing home, or you settle your wages and get your own house."

I felt that a nursing home was not an option, and my attorney was urging me to take the offer. I told him, "That doesn't seem fair to me that we have to settle our wages in order to get a house for us to stay in." But at the same time, I was under a lot of pressure. We were staying at my nephew's house, and his wife was pregnant and unhappy because there was so much traffic going through her house, and she needed her space.

With my back up against the wall, I agreed that we would settle for the wages in order to find a house. An insurance company representative finally said to me, regarding the nursing agency I wanted to have, "Well, I'll tell you what, that nursing agency you want? They want too much money, and we're not going to pay that kind of money, so if you don't want to use the nursing agency that we sent there, you train and hire your own nurses and we'll pay them."

I said "okay" and took on the challenge. I put ads in different hospitals. I realized that because Darien was on the vent, I needed respiratory therapists; eighty percent of his care is respiratory, and if he can't breathe, he can't live. I knew I needed somebody there to keep him from getting pneumonia, because if he got pneumonia, that could take him out.

I knew I needed people there who could keep his airway going and would be able to respond when he coded. So, I started a search for other respiratory therapists and finally found some I felt comfortable with. We came up with a program and hired and trained our own nurses; I don't think I slept for three months while training them. We cross-trained—taught the respiratory therapists how to do the nursing end of Darien's care and taught the nurses how to do the respiratory end of his care.

My sister, Mary, is a perfectionist and a great organizer, and really does not play when it comes to Darien. There were times when I had to remind her who Darien's real mother was, but I thank God for her and could not have survived this without her. All of his nurses are a blessing, and they all love and admire Darien. I have come to trust them explicitly with his life.

After we got the whole program up and running, *six*

years went by. Thank God, to this day, Darien has never had a bed sore because my nurses are so good and take care of Darien so well. He never had any other outside issues come up, either.

After six years, the insurance company decided that I knew what I was doing—Darien had lived for six years, and they were paying out all this money to keep him alive. So, what did they decide to do? They broke up his support system. All of a sudden, on a Friday afternoon, I got a phone call from a woman at a new nursing agency. She said to me, "We've been hired to take over Darien's case." Naturally, I replied, "What do you mean you've been hired to take over Darien's case? I don't need any nurses!"

The woman replied, "The insurance case manager called and hired us today. I'll take the case, but only if you promise me that you will train my nurses to take care of Darien."

I said "no way" because I had stayed up for three months straight training the first set of nurses, and had even had a breakdown due to the lack of sleep. I told her, "I'm not putting myself through that again, training nurses—been there, done that. You know how serious Darien's condition is, and my nurses are fine. Now, if you want to take this case and come in here on Monday, you can do that, but let me say this to you: If anything happens to Darien, I'm coming after you."

So, guess what? They cancelled the contract with

the insurance company! And what was the insurance company's next move in the sick chess game they were playing with Darien's life and my nerves? They fired his nurses! I remember when I asked the company directly, "You're just going to deny him nursing care?" My therapist was making $35 an hour, and the nurses were making $25 an hour. The insurance company said, "Tell you what. You can keep the nurses, but we're knocking their pay down to ten dollars an hour." What respiratory nurse do you know who's going to work for $10 an hour?

***

Nurse Carolyn: There were a bunch of instances where the insurance company didn't want to give us raises, despite how long we'd worked there. I would have stayed on anyway; I love Darien just like a brother and hadn't known what the pay was before I took this job. I just knew he was special and I wanted to be involved in his care.

***

Attorney Jerry Goodmark: My impression of the family was—given that the accident had happened in 1993 and I wasn't seeing them till eight years later—they had incredible strength and courage to keep this gentleman going all that time. My first impression centered on how courageous they were.

Darien's mother, Linda McCoy, was pretty weary at that point because she was basically managing all of Darien's nurses and medical care by herself and wasn't getting a lot of cooperation from the worker's compensation carrier. By that point, she really had battle fatigue, I think, and was thrilled to know that our firm specialized in catastrophic injuries. We would be taking over the brunt of the battle with the insurance company; that this was no longer her function seemed to be a great relief. It was clear to me right from the start that the insurance company was trying to make this as difficult on the family as they could, and that was inconsistent with my history of handling these kinds of cases. Typically, when you have a catastrophically injured patient, the smartest thing for the insurance carrier to do is cooperate and try to make his life as easy as possible, because it keeps their payments down. It's much easier if the patient is doing better, because logically speaking, when he's not doing well, it's going to cost the insurance carrier more money.

I hadn't participated in the first few years of dealing with the insurance company, but as I sat there listening to Ms. McCoy give me a history of her battle, it was inconsistent with what I thought was good practice, and with what I had seen with some other insurance companies. It also surprised me because the original company Darien had been employed with when he'd had his accident was a big hardware corporation and could certainly have afforded the care Darien medically required.

I remember going to their home to meet Darien during our first round of depositions up in Atlanta. Heading into those depositions, I wanted to make sure I had a good idea of what Darien's physical and mental situation was, and so we had quite a few meetings at his home. That gave me the mental impression that his family was caring for him in an exemplary way; he had muscle tone in his body after eight years of being flat on his back, and he couldn't have that unless somebody was being really diligent in physical therapy, massage and every other thing that they could do for him. And his spirit was good, too, which was amazing after eight years in that situation.

My impression after meeting Darien was that he was among the most courageous individuals I'd ever met, and I've met a lot of seriously injured people. I've met people in wheelchairs who are bitter and resentful, and that's typically part of the process they go through. They go through anger then acceptance, but Darien was almost serene in his resolve. It was just obvious that he has tremendous faith.

The attended-care situation with the nurses was probably the biggest challenge I faced in this case, and it's kind of my specialty in worker's comp. Linda was responsible for hiring and firing nurses. In a lot of cases, an insurance company will just hire a service, and the client then doesn't have all the administrative headaches and scheduling problems. But I found out early on that there was a shortage of nurses in the catastrophic-care category, so Linda took the bull by the horns and trained them herself, along with her sister. She is very lucky to have a sister who is a respiratory specialist—Mary Helms, who is a registered nurse and has just been wonderful in training the other nurses. Respiratory care is an extraordinarily complicated form of care giving.

To underscore that point, Dr. Osborne, in the first round of depositions we did, pointed out that Darien was at risk for respiratory failure at any minute—that he could choke on his own aspiration at any second and needed someone who could perform CPR right away. He also pointed out that you simply can't do that with one nurse; you have to have two people. That was simply dictated by his condition. So, right away, we had a very unusual situation wherein I was claiming that Darien was entitled to two twenty-four-hour nurses, and the insurance company certainly was not agreeing to that in any way. They were going to fight that because it was a big-money issue.

As things progressed with the depositions, I made a request for an alternative case manager; we've had five since 2001, when I got involved in the case. The basis for seeking an alternative case manager at that point was rooted in the fact that the woman handling Darien's case was proving difficult to the point where, as far as Linda and I were concerned, she didn't have Darien's best interests at heart. It was clearly Linda's opinion that this case manager would sooner have seen Darien code and die than go on having the company pay his medical bills.

There's no question that Linda felt that threatened, and as far as I'm concerned, she was justified because these people—the case managers—are hired by the insurance company and basically do the company's bidding. They're supposed to be objective and independent, but many times that isn't true. And the latter was definitely true with this case manager.

Eventually, we got her replaced and had yet another case manager who didn't seem to have Darien's best interest at heart—Judy Mehl, who proved to be the most difficult, and whose deposition was just bizarre. She was the most egregious in my view, and we eventually got rid of her. I took Judy's deposition in November 2001 in an effort to get her removed, and as with anything in worker's comp cases, I had to ask for it first from the insurance company. If they voluntarily do it, that's as far as it goes. If they deny your request, you file a petition with the court, a pretrial is set, and then you get the judge eventually.

That was what happened here. We filed a case for an alternative manager, and after I took her second deposition on December 4, 2002, the judge eventually took her off the case. That was just one of a hundred fights we've had with the insurance company in the course of this case. They didn't like it; they had to hire a new case manager as the judge had awarded, and thereafter fought us on many other issues. Looking at our first set of issues from the pretrial, dated March 2, 2002, there are thirty-six issues listed in the complaint.

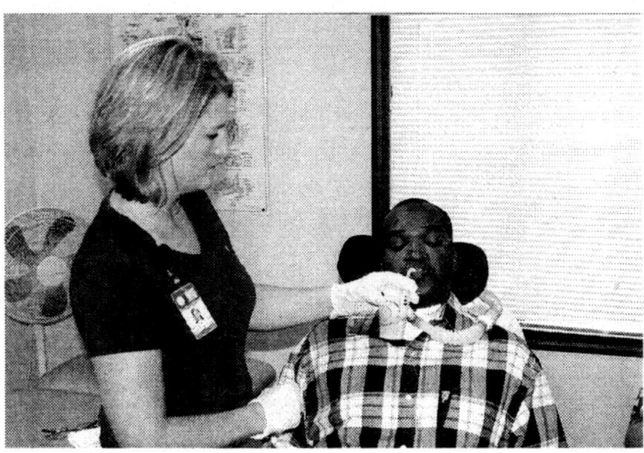

Marie and Darien

Chapter 17

So that we may boldly say, The Lord is my helper, and I will not fear what man shall do unto me.
—Hebrews 13:6

Auntie Dee, Darien and Auntie Missie

Amid dealing with all of these issues, I was in the process of building a handicap-accessible home with the money we got from our wage settlement. Once the house was completed, all I had to do was brick it in and pick out my appliances.

Just before I could do that, however, the insurance company knocked the nurses' wages down to $10 and hour. It was a true case of sabotage. That was Darien's lifeline—I could not lose my nurses! So, what did I do with the rest of the money I had in the bank instead of finishing the house? I met the payroll myself and made up the difference in what they didn't pay the nurses.

The offenses by the insurance carrier against Darien as a patient were stacking up. Surely, they felt the odds were too against him, but I was determined to beat them and persevere. To do so, I had to sell that house, take the proceeds and fight the insurance company in court. It took eleven months, and I had to come up with $18,000 a month to meet my payroll for almost a year in order to keep Darien alive. But I want to tell you that there is a God in heaven. When I got down to that last month and my last $18,000 in the bank, I told Darien, "I don't know how we're going to make it. We're down to our last pennies." And that day, I got a phone call letting me know that we had been granted an emergency hearing before the judge. I had been flying back and forth to and from Miami all that time, going to court to battle the insurance company.

Another turnaround for us during this period came with my finding out that when the insurance company had cut Darien's nurses pay down to $10, they had facilitated that by going to Emory Hospital, where Darien was receiving his therapy. They had told his doctor, Dr. Grisom to write a prescription for the insurance company to get rid of the nurses that Darien had! When I found this out, I went to the medical board and threatened to get Dr. Grisom's license pulled, and I won because I'd gone to the library and found a case like Darien's where they'd said that it was absolutely necessary for him to have twenty-four/seven respiratory care. Thank God I found it.

I took it to our lawyer, and when we got to the doctor's deposition, the lawyer showed him that and said, "I got your license right here in my hand." And that was when the doctor did a three-sixty on the insurance company: He got scared and changed his testimony. He told the medical board that the case manager had pressured him and told him he had to do it. Then he said, "Not only does Darien need nursing respiratory twenty-four/seven, but he needs *two* nurses."

And that was how I was able to get two nurses around the clock for him. What was meant for evil actually turned around for Darien's good, because the doctor ended up saying that Darien needed two nurses per shift, so we won that and got it written in stone. Having two nurses was a blessing from God, and this freed me up to have a life. I had to learn how to live again as best I could. Still, I knew it wasn't over yet.

***

Attorney Jerry Goodmark: The biggest issue in

that first 2002 complaint was number nineteen, which requested an additional twenty-four hours of nursing care. That meant two nurses on duty all the time, which was very controversial because all the doctors did *not* testify to that. There was conflict about that.

But Darien's main treating doctor, Dr. Osborn, testified to it. Then, I had to go to the experts at Shepherd's Center, who were basically on the insurance company's side, and take their depositions and prove that CPR could not be done on this kind of patient by just one nurse. I had to prove that Darien would die if anyone tried to do CPR with one nurse, because one person has to bag him and the other has to do chest compression, and one person can't do that.

I'll never forget when I was taking Dr. Leslie's deposition. He was the main doctor at Shepherd's at the time. "Well, doctor, can one person do this?" I asked. "Have you done it?" And he said, "Yeah, for about a minute."

"How many people come in when you have a crash code?" I asked then.

He responded, "Oh, we have four people on the crash cart."

Even their experts testified for us on that issue eventually, but it certainly was no slam dunk. In addition to a number of trials, we've had a number of mediations, which are settlement conferences. The way this case goes, things change depending on Darien's condition. The consistent challenge has been dealing with the insurance company, definitely.

***

Miraculously, on the way down to Miami, I got a phone call from my attorney. He said, "Guess what, Linda? You can turn around. They folded—they gave in. They're going to pay you back for the difference in the wages you've been paying your nurses this last year. The judge ordered them to do that and ordered them to pay you interest on all the money you've paid out."

Everything went back to normal until that terrible day when, after six years of not coding, Darien's nurse, who was getting him ready for church, began yelling, "Linda, come quick, I need you!" I ran downstairs and there it was, happening again: Darien coded. We worked until he came to. I found myself in a state of literal panic; I'd thought I would never see that happen again, and after six years, I couldn't believe it was happening all over again.

Amazingly, in a testament to my son's belief and faith in God, even after that, he told the nurse to finish getting him dressed to go to church! I begged Darien to stay home, afraid it would happen again, but he insisted, so I gave in. He, his brother and his nurse went to church after all that. I was so nervous, I went to my garden to pick collard greens, saying to myself, "I can never take this for granted again." Fear washed over me because I realized he could code at any time, in any place. As the fear engulfed me, I became overwhelmed.

When Darien got home from church, I was still in the garden, and he, in an effort to get back to normal as quickly for all of us as possible, sent his brother to ask me if he could go to the mall. I begged him not to go, but Darien, being the warrior he is, was determined not to let anything stop him from living his life. I was afraid for him, but knowing in my heart that we could not live in fear, I let him go.

When Darien's van pulled back in the driveway and he flashed me one of his big smiles, it reminded me of the most important factor in all of this: that Darien has been determined to live his life no matter what, and he never let anything stop him from doing whatever he wanted to do.

***

Nurse Carolyn: Transportation got easier when Darien got a van. Then, he started going out on the weekends. He had routine places he went where people knew him. When we go out, Darien has a wheelchair and a driver for his van, and either Dee or I go with him in case he needs to be suctioned. He has a TV that he watches in the back of the van, and we've even gone on a couple road trips. We've been trying to get Darien to go on vacation for years, and we did go to Miami one year and flew on a private jet. We had an ambulance waiting when we got to the airport, and they drove us to his grandmother's house, which he got a big kick out of.

There's always a team that goes with him when he goes out. He goes to movies, and one nurse drives and the other sits in the back with Darien in case he needs assistance with suctioning or whatever else. He has a television in his van, and if he wants to watch a certain program, we turn the channel for him. Now, he's broadened his horizons some, if you want to call it that: He goes to church every Sunday if the weather permits, and after church, he may want to go to WalMart or the pet store to get fish for his tank. When we're there, we might buy new fish or watch a dog show if they're doing training.

Darien goes out a lot now, and the only thing that is wrong with him is that he can't walk and breathe on his own at this point. Other than that, he has his mind and can tell you what he wants—and he knows what he wants.

Part V
The Long Road Back

Chapter 18

I will say of the Lord, He is my refuge and my fortress, my God, and in Him will I trust.

—Psalms 91:2

Cousin Al Jenkins and Darien

After that, because I had sold the house to meet payroll, the house we were living in was not equipped for Darien. There was one way in and one way out, and he was staying in the basement. I had always looked for houses with basements because in Georgia, with the storms we have, the safest place to be is the basement. I had set up a basement apartment for Darien so he'd be safe.

The house we were in at that time didn't have enough emergency exits. A storm had actually come while we were in this particular house, and I had been asking the insurance company for a generator because Darien can't be without power, with all his respiratory equipment. And sure enough, a storm came and knocked out the house's power. The nurse and I were giving Darien breath with bags, and we called 911. We were actually riding in the ambulance through the storm to the emergency room—Darien, the nurse and I—and we got to Southern Regional Hospital. We were without power for three days, and the hospital actually kept trying to get me to take him home because they felt that there was nothing physically wrong with him that they could help with. They said he was taking up a bed in intensive care, if you can believe that.

And I kept saying, "What do you want me to do, bring him home with no power? If I do that, he's going to die."

I was crazy there. I called the power company and let them know Darien was there and had an injury and we ended up being the last people in the neighborhood to get our power back. Everybody else had theirs up the same day; we had to wait three. I was livid, and went over my attorney's head and wrote a letter to the judge myself. Judge Kuker got pissed, called the insurance company himself, and told them they had so many hours to get a generator to my house. It finally showed up.

***

Nurse Carolyn: I think one of the scariest times we went through from a medical vantage point was when the power went out at the old house due to a terrible storm. Linda had been fighting with the insurance company over getting a generator for Darien, because we knew a situation like that could arise. His ventilator will only run for so long before it will turn off, and if we didn't have a generator, Darien's life would be in danger.

And sure enough, when the power did go out, we had to call 911 and spend a week at the hospital. His own team of nurses was taking care of him at the hospital, because we always travel with him—I don't care where we go. The hospital nurses did what they needed to do as far as the machines and everything were concerned, but we did all of the personal care; we were there to do that on all four shifts.

We were there a week before power was restored at home. That type of thing has been life-threatening to Darien for years, and that was another thing that was stressing Linda out—

knowing that something like that was needed to save his life, and that the insurance company wouldn't provide it for him.

***

Darien's aunt/head homecare nurse: I was most worried about the insurance company getting the things Darien needed to live a quality life, one where he could be independent. If he couldn't get the equipment to allow him to be independent, he couldn't have a high-quality life, even though despite having to depend on others, his quality of life was good. For me, that was the biggest issue I'd had with the insurance company denying things that would help Darien live a good life. For instance, Darien likes to go on the computer, and he has male nurses who like to go on and watch sports and YouTube and whatnot. But if he doesn't have a computer, he's just sitting there watching the TV all day.

***

Linda McCoy: Other life-threatening incidents that truly scared us have happened since Darien's accident. One involved Darien getting a new wheelchair after ten years of waiting. Ironically, the left arm of the chair was not adjusted correctly and it was applying pressure to Darien's forearm, which caused a blood clot to form. This put Darien's life in danger.

Dr. Osborne started aggressive treatment for the blood clot with blood thinners, fearing the clot would travel to Darien's lung. During the course of the treatment, Darien started bleeding internally. His stomach became the size of a beach ball. I became very concerned and insisted he be taken to the emergency room. When we arrived, after they did X-rays, the doctors told me that the bleeding in Darien's stomach was so bad, they were afraid to send him to a trauma center, fearing he couldn't handle the ride. They were afraid to move from the emergency room to the intensive care unit as well. It was very serious.

I immediately went into my spiritual mode and told Darien what the doctors said, and we started singing spiritual songs. Darien began moving his lips and singing along with me. We must have sang for an hour straight, not caring who heard us. We kept singing until finally, transportation came and moved Darien to intensive care.

Darien underwent six blood transfusions while he was hospitalized. I insisted they keep him there until his blood count was back to normal, and the whole process took a week. After he was released and sent back home, Darien's nurses and I continued to work to keep his blood count at its normal level, and thankfully, he recovered.

During another incident, Darien's blood pressure kept jumping all over the place. He kept breaking out in cold sweats, and we couldn't get his pressure under control. Finally, he saw his neurologist, Dr. Foot, who said he had to have a procedure to correct his urinary flow.

This was scary because as it turned out, it was a very bloody procedure, but Darien came through it like the champion he is. Thankfully, he has not had any other major incidents since. We have truly been blessed that Darien's overall health since the accident has been excellent. His doctors have called this incredible, phenomenal and even unbelievable. One of his doctors cried a river when he examined Darien and found he was healthy. God has been so faithful in keeping Darien safe and healthy.

***

Among my worst nightmares in dealing with the bone collectors from various insurance companies were their adjustors. One of them, whom we'll call the Angel of Death, suggested that I was crazy for requesting adequate housing for our family because he felt as though Darien was going to die, and that it was absolutely irrational for me to be looking for a house instead of a tombstone. In an even more egregious instance, another adjuster, Gloria Dyer, suggested that the motive behind my seeking the best possible housing for my son was not rooted in my having his best interest at heart, but rather because, as she so eloquently articulated to one of Darien's case managers, I was an ***UPPITY NIGGER*** wanting to live in a nicer house.

One of my greatest victories was winning the court battle for remodification of our home, which resulted in Darien having greater accessibility to areas of his home beyond just the basement for the first time. Previously, he'd been confined to one room in our basement.

Darien has had eight case managers through the insurance company, all of whom wanted to put Darien in a nursing home. Each time one of them mentioned it, I kicked them off the case.

The last case manager who came to see Darien saw the house we were living in and was trying to use it as an excuse to put Darien in a nursing home. She said to me, "You'd better find somewhere to put him other than here, or I'm gonna put him in a nursing home, because this house is a death trap."

Finally, I sold that house and got us into a new home using the settlement the insurance company had had to pay me over the nurses' wages. It had a daylight basement, and that same case manager said she thought it would be adequate. The insurance company still had to come and finish the basement to make it handicap-accessible; we moved into that house in 2000, and they didn't finish the basement until 2006. In sum, it took fifteen years for us to get that insurance company to do right by Darien in terms of the housing.

***

Attorney Jerry Goodmark: One of the huge issues in this case was modification of the home. Darien basically was a prisoner in his own room because the home was not modified. Linda had bought this particular house because it had a wide-open basement that could be modified, and I made a claim for that in April of 2001. If you can believe it, even though the judge awarded them in April of 2003, it was not become completed till 2007.

So there we had a man who had not been able to take a shower since his accident—and couldn't until we had the home modifications done. That was just one small example of what they had to put up with. Home modification was a big, big issue that we won. Judge Kuker was the judge on this case from the beginning and knows more about it than any jurist could. He is a no-nonsense judge who is very fair, and was *always* fair with Darien. Even when he has not awarded us, for the most part, he's always had Darien's best interests at heart. I have had no complaints with Judge Kuker ever.

***

Judge Kuker was very wise and compassionate when it came to Darien. I thank God for him. He even paid me the compliment one day of saying he thought I was doing a great job taking care of Darien, and that Darien was very lucky to have a mother like me. Judge Kuker has been with us on Darien's case for sixteen years. To this day, I don't understand what they mean by the expression "wouldn't any mother do the same?" His answer would always be, "No, not every mother."

Every time it seemed like we got one issue settled with the insurance company, another would arise. After they couldn't get us with the house, they stopped paying for Darien's respiratory and medical supplies for two years, and we had to fight them on that. It just so happened that I had favor with the people at the respiratory and medical supply companies, both of whom had come over and met Darien. They liked me and saw my struggle, and they promised me that as long as Darien lived, he would have everything that he needed. For two years, Heart Medical Supply gave Darien everything he needed—his medicines and so on—without pay. The respiratory company did the same thing.

We have had many nightmares with the insurance companies handling Darien's case—so many, we cannot count them all. In spite of all of our trials, we still have faith in God and the people He has put in our lives. We will continue to fight for Darien's life, and God will always protect Darien and keep him safe so he will fulfill his purpose in life. I am confident of that. There is a reason for all of our struggles, and they will not be in vain.

Darien eight years old

Chapter 19

Train up a child in the way he should go: and when he is old, he will not depart from it.

—Proverbs 22:6

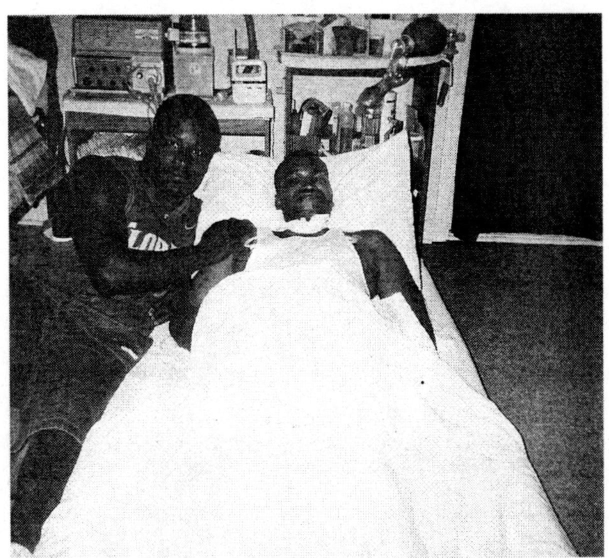

Magnus and Darien

While I know that Darien has appreciated my fighting our battles with the insurance companies and medical professionals, I've tried never to lose sight of the fact that in the end, these are his battles above anyone else's. He's the first one who had to make the decision to go on fighting;

he called the first shot that ignited our fight for his life. And as we were finally beginning to win some victories in that battle with the insurance companies, I felt it was equally important that Darien be able to feel his voice was heard in the course of those struggles.

To that end, we found a wonderful therapist to work with Darien on developing more of a voice of his own, and through their hard work together, that's exactly what we achieved!

***

Dr. Marinson: I was called in for two reasons, to help with two different sets of matters. One was Darien's profound depression; when I met him he was coping with his limitations patiently, like he had from the beginning, but his inability to be able to speak was very frustrating to him. It made him feel cut off from everybody. Not only was he confined to his wheelchair, but he was also prevented from being able to even have the human freedom of expression by speaking to us from that chair.

My first focus when our sessions started was being comfortable in a room with him. I don't deal with quadriplegics on a regular basis, and I experienced a little dread for quite a while, every time I would go to see him. My impression was that Darien was acutely aware of how people responded to him and was incredibly gracious in focusing his effort on making those other people comfortable. Darien does this to a fault.

He feels guilty about the stress he's put his mother through, so he tries to hold in when he's upset so she can't see it. But, a lot of times, she does anyway, and that was a major part of what I was working on with him in the beginning. It was a joint effort because both Darien and his mother, Linda, attended the sessions. To communicate, I would ask him yes-or-no questions and he would blink once for yes, twice for no. One of our focuses became finding a broader array of communication options for him.

As I said earlier, one of the reasons why I was brought in was that Darien was depressed. The second reason was that the insurance company was fighting against his doctors, who had prescribed a piece of equipment that could be used with a computer to enable Darien to write out letters and be able to communicate with us verbally—with his eye movements, if I remember correctly. He would have been able to actually express himself verbally.

Part of my purpose in seeing him was to document the medical necessity of this equipment for him in terms of his psychological need not to be isolated in his body. It sounds ridiculous to have to explain this to somebody, but when you're fighting lawyers who are fighting to keep the insurance company from having to pay, you have to dot your I's and cross your T's and provide medical information that will stand up as evidence in a court of law.

***

Darien's aunt/head homecare nurse: When you're around a person all the time, you can tell when they feel depressed. When Darien went out and people looked at him, sometimes that would make him feel very uncomfortable. He had to get to a point where he looked past it, which he does now. But back in the beginning, he would get depressed about things that were going on or that he wanted to have done. We had to deal with the insurance company to supply us with the means to make things happen, and they were slow about doing it, and things like that would make Darien feel down and get depressed. He felt that if he had a particular thing, he'd be able to do something he wanted.

When that happened, I had my ways. I would read him a little scripture from the Bible and we would talk about it, or we'd watch movies like *The Five Heartbeats* or *The Temptations*—different things to take his mind off of his problems. I'd play music for him as well, and those things would kind of pick him up.

We also listened to healing tapes. Darien was very spiritual, and he'd put one on and it just seemed to take him away mentally, which was important because you have to be there mentally to hold yourself there physically.

***

Dr. Marinson: Ironically, in the course of our initial meetings, something—as Linda would say—miraculous occurred. Darien began expressing himself to me directly. As our sessions went on, we were becoming friends, establishing a better and better rapport, and I could say whatever came to my mind, being very open and real with him from moment to moment. I think he was getting a kick out of our meetings.

I'm a lot looser in general because I'm a therapist, and because of the kind of therapist I am. I'm sixty years old and was into the counterculture, and was trained in what's called experiential psychotherapy, where you use your own persona—who you are in that moment—and your own reactions to be therapeutic just by being yourself. It sounds simple but involves a radical honesty that in practice can be difficult, because you can't just be polite.

People were always hiding things from Darien, and that was hurting him. It made him feel more isolated, so I was honest with him about the horror I experienced working with him, and we would talk about that together. It was very painful, even gut wrenching, but we got through it with a combination of humor and Darien's incredible spirit. God has blessed him with incredible powers to keep his spirit strong in spite of the extremity of his physical limitations, which became spiritual limitations in terms of his not being able to communicate with other human beings. But we were communicating a lot within those limitations.

Darien was becoming more and more enthusiastic about being able to talk to me. So, somebody came up with the idea that he could speak through his respirator by timing it. He could say a few words each time the air blew a certain way through him. It was in my office that Darien spoke his first words that way, and I'll never forget that day. Linda, of course, was full of uncontrollable tears of joy for granting his miracle, and that was an early turning point in his therapy with me.

That gave me a more ambitious agenda with Darien, though it didn't expand from there in any linear fashion because to this day, we can never count from meeting to meeting on how well he's going to be able to speak. His medical condition is so extreme that even something like congestion can interfere, so we never know whether it's going to be an easy day or a very frustrating day for speaking.

Still, we had two main areas of focus. One was his outrage over the evildoing on the part of the worker's compensation people and the fact that they had forced him to go back to work with his neck injury, setting him up for the fall that made him quadriplegic. As a result of that, our second area of focus was the fact that this was a young man who was devoted to his mother and saw what her devotion to him was doing to her life. There was a lot of outrage, and to be able to express that verbally instead of just blinking his eyes was huge, obviously. He was then able to articulate in his own words, with dignity, his outrage.

I hope you will get a chance in this book to hear his own expressions of outrage, because in the mean-spirited world in which we live, it's rare that you have an opportunity to hear someone with the caliber of spiritual beauty of Darien Smith's soul express in beautiful English a *whole* lot of anger—though in a language that is never harsh to God's ears.

***

Nurse Carolyn: At first, our biggest challenge was communication. We could only lip read, which is still my preferred form of communication. We're trained at Shepherd's to do that, and we have made that the routine for the other nurses that work with Darien. That works out fine; it's not very hard. Some words we can get, and some we can't. When we can't, that's when we ask him to spell. Other times, we deflate his cuff, which is what we do when he goes to speech therapy, in which he's doing quite well.

Beyond speech, deflating his cuff also allows him to eat some and drink some, taking sips, and exercise with his tongue and do words. That hadn't developed till recently into a full-blown eating process, so we're just making sure he's swallowing well and that he's not aspirating, that the food is not going down into his lungs. That could cause major problems, especially with his being on a ventilator, so we always make sure no food or liquids get down into his lungs.

When we asked Darien what he wanted to eat, he said he didn't know because it had been so long. We're doing apple sauce and water right now, and we put dye in it to make sure he doesn't aspirate; we can suction him out and look to see if there's any dye blocking his passage and suction that out.

***

Darien's aunt/head homecare nurse: Darien

has what you would call an artificial airway in his trachea, and it has a cuff on it that we can inflate, and that keeps a whole lot of foreign matter from getting down in to Darien's lungs. With his not being able to swallow effectively, he can run the risk of aspiration, so with the cuff, we leave it up. But if we let that cuff down, he can talk some.

When he first came home, he couldn't do that, so we communicated through lip reading. I was already trained in lip reading and how to let his cuff down so he could talk. When he can speak depends on whether he has a lot of secretions; he can't control all of them at will. If there are too many, he won't be able to speak as well if we put the cuff down, so we try to keep the secretions under control to allow him to be able to speak.

He's also going to speech therapy and is being taught how to control his secretions and when to swallow. When he gets full control his secretions, its going to allow him to speak better. He's also got something in the oven now—he's going to be able to operate the computer himself.

***

Dr. Marinson: As our communication process improved, two other things we worked through in therapy were his sadness for his mother and his sadness for himself over everything he's lost.

We also looked at how he has grown spiritually through his struggle. For example, I teach people to use meditation and prayer to calm their nervous systems when they're upset, and to control the pain. With my other patients, I'll have them make a fist to put all that stress reaction, all the anger, all the upset that keeps them from being able to feel close to God, in some part of their body, in their muscles. That helps them keep focused on talking to God instead of having their own evil thoughts interfere.

Darien is not physically capable of doing that, but he can create a focus in his mind on a visual image of a duck swimming in the lake that his house overlooks, and he can hold that image in his mind to help him pay attention and not be distracted by all the turmoil inside. That is one of the things we've worked on.

His progress really began with being able to speak early on in our work together. The culmination of this came last fall with President Obama's candidacy. Darien decided that it was time for him to get beyond the confines of that wheelchair and the room in which he's stuck. He wanted to get more involved in the world by getting registered to vote. He was so happy all last fall, wearing Obama T-shirts and feeling again like he was part of life and what was going on in the world. Actually being able to get out and vote, to express himself that way, was a sign of how far he'd come from just being an invalid locked up in a room.

Linda, when I first met her, was a nervous wreck, and she freely admitted that she was. The strain on her from dealing with fighting the insurance companies—it reminded me of that Danny Devito/ Matt Damon movie *The Rainmaker*. She was like the mother in that movie: strained to the max, to the point where there were times when she came across like a total basket case.

But she uses her faith to pull herself together miraculously, and is able to be a very strong vocal advocate for Darien. She wisely saw, however, that her son wouldn't fully recover his manhood unless she stopped doing everything for him. In the beginning, she had to be in the room more often than not just so that we could communicate, and so when he was able to start speaking for himself, it was an obviously tremendous breakthrough. We all realized that this provided Darien with an opportunity to speak with me privately, without needing his mother's assistance.

Naturally, that changed the dialogue Darien and I had, especially with regard to his concerns about his mother and his own emotional distress in terms of how upset he was. He was able to cry when she wasn't around, but wouldn't have before then because he didn't want her to see how upset he was. Some doctors would tell you that this breakthrough might have helped save his life. His being able to vent meant there was less of a burden on his mother; the more he was able to recover from his depression, the less she had to worry about.

He and I had some great sessions themed around how thrilled we were that our combined outrage about the evils of corporate tyranny were finally having a chance to be addressed. I think Darien feels like something of an activist; very much, I think that's one of the things that's keeping him alive. The world needs to know what was done to him so it won't be done to others, and because of his strong spiritual presence, his faith, he is able to articulate this with such dignity. The heart of even the most cynical person in America, someone who might disagree with his politics, can be pierced by his words.

My impression is that ultimately, I'm not sure the question of whether he'll walk again matters to Darien at all. He feels God's presence all the time, and he and I agree that there are a lot of things we don't know about what God can do and is going to do. I do know that Darien has not given up hope that he might be able to use his legs again. Whether God is going to make that happen or not is up to

God, and Darien is able to accept that. It's my view that God uses science to make things happen, but we both know that it's in His hands, not ours.

I feel that we've accomplished a lot of what we initially needed to get him into a better headspace about living day to day. At this point in our relationship, I pretty much wait on him; I don't have an agenda for Darien in terms of what I think he needs to accomplish with me. I did in the beginning, but I see him as a fully functioning human being who is psychologically healthier than most people. There are times when his circumstances make it difficult for him to sustain his emotional well-being. Those are the times when he calls on me.

Chapter 20

> And the Lord turned the captivity of Job, when he prayed for his friends; also the Lord gave Job twice as much as he had before.
>
> —Job 42:10

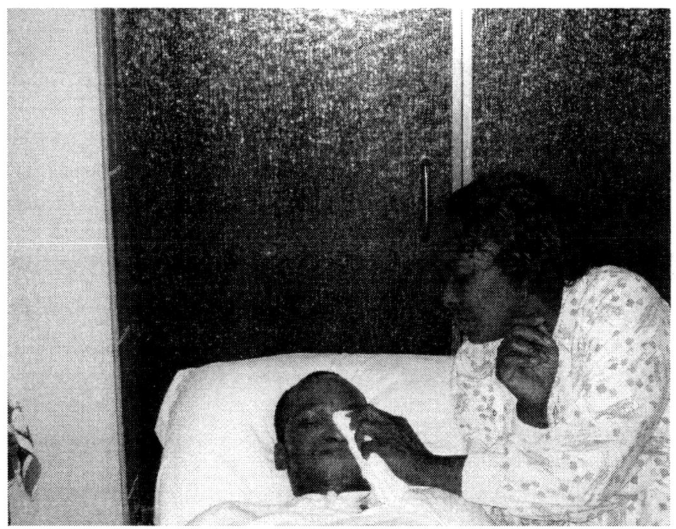

Darien and Angela

I raised my younger son, Cameron, through all of this. He was an honor student since kindergarten, is gifted in music and is just a really, really brilliant young man. He got a scholarship to Duke and another to West Point and all of these prominent schools, but he turned them all down and went to Mercer so he could come home on the weekends to be with his brother, and he has not missed a weekend to this day.

Every weekend since he has been in Macon, he comes home and spends time with his brother. He has one more semester to go; he is majoring in business and is on the debate team. I'm just a very fortunate, very blessed woman.

In his sophomore year, Cameron went a little wild, and he gave us a grandson at the age of nineteen—Cameron J. Clemons II, a.k.a. "CJ," born January 3, 2006. At eleven months old, he watched the nurses take care of Darien and suctioned Darien's mouth. He thinks he's the nurse.

Little CJ is so fortunate to experience the love Darien and Cameron and I have to offer. And it is a gift from the most high to be able to instill the values that Darien has help us all develop into Cameron J. Clemons II. He took a liking to Darien and there's a super bond there. It shows me what a wonderful father we still believe Darien will be one day.

Darien attended all of his brother's basketball games, sometimes buying shoes for the entire team and lending his van for transportation when needed. I was the team's personal cheerleader. One day, CJ asked me, "Mom, why do you have to buy Gatorade for the entire team and cheer for everyone on the team? No other parent does this but you." He didn't understand till one day, after a game, his teammate, Nathan, came to me and said, "Thank you, Ms. Linda, for cheering for me. You don't know how good you make me feel when you call my name. Every time I hear you call my name, I hear my mother's voice. She died two months ago of cancer."

Tears welled up, and I felt so overwhelmed. When we got home that night, I looked at CJ and said, "Now, do you see? You never know who you are helping just by being unselfish."

Darien pays for CJ's education at Mercer University and has high hopes for his brother, who feels like he can't let Darien down. It hasn't been easy for Cameron; he has had to grow up fast as he is now a father as well, and I'm so proud he didn't leave his responsibility. He stuck with the young lady, attended all the doctor's visits, was there when his son was born, and makes sure his son is taken care of. I feel so blessed for that because Cameron's dad was not around for him in his formative years, and he is determined to make sure that is not his path. CJ calls me "Me-ma." I won't get started on CJ or this book will never end.

Cam, my nephew, is an EMT and captain in the Atlanta Fire Department. He was there from the very beginning, taking classes at Shepherd's Spinal Center and being a friend to Darien in his time of need. He later took us into his home till we found a place of our own. I named my second son, Cameron, after my nephew in tribute to his dedication to our family and his compassion and commitment to us. As a matter of fact, in my last month of pregnancy with CJ, my nephew, Cameron, was there by my side. He took me to the emergency room. I felt honored to name my son after my nephew.

***

Nurse Carolyn: In Darien's area of the house, there's a room for CJ and when he comes to visit, he stays there so he can be down here with his brother. They interact and do things together while he's home. Darien also loves being an uncle to his little nephew; he loves him to death, and loves his nephew comes to visit and helps suction him and tries to help us get him in the bed. It's just wonderful; he has great support.

Both CJ and his son are there quite often, and it excites Darien to know they're coming for a visit. He enjoys it when they're there. When Darien's out and knows CJ's son needs something, he'll go shopping for him, buy toys for him—he's just a great uncle.

Between CJ and Darien, there's a great rapport. CJ listens to Darien just like Darien is his dad; because there's so much of an age difference, Darien takes on something of a father-figure role. When Darien talks to CJ about anything, he listens and talks to him like a father and there's a lot of mutual respect there.

***

While we were waging battle on one hand with the

worker's comp insurance carrier, I had begun another battle to sue the company Darien had worked for when his accident had happened. Money was not my goal, but I knew it was the only way to exact any measure for my son, to make them pay for the literal hell they had put our family through. I remember when they were refusing housing for Darien, I took Darien and the nurses and picketed in front of their corporate offices in downtown Atlanta. We marched up and down the street with signs.

On our way home, I said to Darien, "Don't feel despondent. Don't feel discouraged." And all of a sudden, an idea popped into my head, and I said "No, we're not going to quit, we're not quitters. You know what, Darien? You need some light bulbs in your room. So we're going home, and we're going to put your apron on, and we're going to go to that store and get you some light bulbs."

Technically, he was still an employee with the company. So, I put his apron on and rolled him into the store, and of course, everybody was looking at him in his wheelchair, with this respirator and apron on. And all of these employees were walking up to him and looking at him, and I asked them to get the manager, to whom I said, "I want you to meet my son, Darien Smith. He is an employee of this company, and he fell and was hurt. This is a home-improvement company, yet you all refuse to give him adequate housing. What I want you to do is get on the phone right now and call the corporate office, and tell them that Darien Smith and his mother are in your store."

If I'd had to visit every store in Atlanta, I would have done it, and I would have told every employee, "This is what you have to look forward to if you get hurt on this job, with this company."

This was in response to what had hurt Darien the most: He'd been so dedicated to them, and when he'd needed them, they had turned their back on him.

***

Attorney Jerry Goodmark: Worker's comp is supposed to be an exclusive remedy against an employer. In other words, an employer that gets worker's comp insurance and makes himself subject to it is not subject to any other kind of lawsuit. However, there's a case called Aguilera that says there's an exception in the law wherein if the employer acts badly and does things that compromise the health, safety and welfare of individuals—and the employer knows it—then you can sue the employer as well as handle the worker's comp case.

When I looked at Darien's case, I said, "If there has *ever* been a case where Aguilera might apply, it's this one." From there, I referred it to the firm of Ritchie-Leopold, and the attorney who handled the case over there was Ted Leopold.

I acted as Ted's point man in the sense that I provided evidence of everything he alleged that the employer and insurance company had done to Darien. He was able to use all my depositions and then make his own conclusions in the complaint he filed.

***

Civil Attorney Ted Leopold: I've been practicing for more than twenty years, and in 1995, I began litigating a specialty that later became referred to as "managed care" cases. At the time, there were very few if any of them. The case I took on was a complaint against Humana for a denial of care to a child with cerebral palsy; in 2000, I tried that case, and it was one of the first managed-care cases to go to trial in the country. We won, and it ended up being the largest punitive-damage award for an individual in Florida. The jury awarded $80 million to this child due to Humana's outrageous conduct.

Since 2001, managed-care litigation has evolved, but there are still very few people who do it in the country. Up until two or three years ago in Florida, you couldn't sue a worker's comp carrier. But then, a Florida Supreme Court ruling on another case,

Aquilar, came out. It said that if the worker's comp carrier acted egregiously, they can be sued for intentional infliction of emotional distress.

In terms of misconduct of carriers, Darien's case was certainly one of the worst I've seen. My first impression was that Darien's mother, Linda, was a very educated, bright and sophisticated client. There's nothing like a mother-child bond, and without Linda McCoy as his advocate, Darien would not even be alive today. She refused to give up and insisted that everything and anything be done in order to provide justice for her son. She truly was the engine behind it all, and when I talked to her for the very first time, it was obvious this was a case that needed to be filed.

Darien's case is historically interesting because when we originally filed his case, the Florida Supreme Court ruling had not yet been decided, so Darien's case was stayed by the judge while we waited to see what would happen in the Florida Supreme Court case. Once the Supreme Court ruled that the worker's comp carriers could be sued, we proceeded with the suit. Two years elapsed between when I met Linda and Darien and filed their suit and when that Supreme Court case was decided. Darien was getting basic worker's comp benefits, but that was it. His condition was horrible because he was a C-1 ventilator quad and all he could do was blink his eyes to communicate. It doesn't get any worse than that.

Once we filed the case, we litigated the hell out of it through depositions, discovery and so on. Still, nothing happened during those two years we were waiting on the Florida Supreme Court. Once we moved ahead following their ruling and jumpstarted the case, Linda's main concern was to provide a full measure of justice for Darien. All we can do in our system is monetary recovery, so I was trying to obtain that for him for the outrageous and egregious acts of the worker's comp carrier and the third-party administrator of that carrier.

***

Linda and Darien brought a case against U.S.A., Inc., the National Union Fire Insurance Company of Pittsburgh, PA, Gab Robins North American, Inc., and Sedgwick CMS, Inc. Seeking damages that exceeded $15,000 exclusive of interest and costs, the allegations included:

- From at least February 1998 until March 2000, Defendants National Union and GAB, acting as agents for ***, engaged in a campaign of intentional tortuous conduct that they knew or should have known would cause Plaintiff Darien Smith to suffer severe emotional distress and or risk of physical injury or death.

- Defendants' campaign consisted of manipulating, depriving, denying, and unreasonably delaying medically necessary and life-preserving care to Darien Smith.
- Defendants took such tortuous actions without any justification and for the sole purpose of increasing their profits by avoiding expenditures for care undeniably due Darien Smith.
- Defendants' tortuous campaign began as early as February 1998 when Defendant GAB, by and through its agents and employees, arbitrarily and without notice fired all of Darien Smith's attending nurses and decreed that they would be replaced.
- This decision was taken even though:
    - these nurses had cared for Darien Smith for 3 ½ years and had therefore become expert in keeping him safe and alive;
    - these nurses had learned to communicate with Darien despite his inability to speak;
    - these nurses had become Darien's close friends; and
    - the new nurses hired by Defendants did not have sufficient training or experience to provide the necessary care for Darien Smith.
- The sole reason for Defendants' firing of Darien Smith's nurses was their refusal to pay these nurses a reasonable, living wage for their work.

• These cold, callous actions intentionally or recklessly caused Darien Smith to suffer severe emotional distress, and subjected him to risk of severe physical injury or death..

• Defendants' campaign continued in April 1998. At that time, Defendant GAB, by and through its agents and employees, improperly pressured one of Darien Smith's treating physicians, Dr. Samuel P. Grissom, not to prescribe 24-hour skilled respiratory care for Darien Smith and instead to prescribe only a Registered Nurse for eight hours per day, and a non-professional for 16 hours per day. Dr. Grissom wrote the prescription as requested by GAB.

• Defendant GAB's efforts to get Dr. Grissom not to provide 24-hour respiratory care were unwarranted, outrageous, and extremely dangerous to the health and life of Darien Smith.

• Because of his condition and dependence on a ventilator to breathe, Darien Smith regularly develops mucus plugs in his respiratory tubes. If Darien is not closely monitored, and these plugs are not diligently removed through suction, Darien could asphyxiate in minutes. In addition, Darien must be taken off his respirator when these mucus plugs are removed. Without a skilled respiratory therapist available, Darien could easily go into respiratory arrest from which he would be unable to recover.

• Despite the importance of 24-hour skilled respiratory care for Darien Smith, Defendant GAB sought to deprive him of such care and thereby gravely jeopardized his health and life.

• But Defendants' egregious tortuous campaign against Darien Smith did not end here.

• From at least March to May 1999, Defendant GAB, as agent for Defendants AIG and ***, repeatedly refused to pay for Darien Smith's medically-necessary nursing care.

• And in June 1999, Defendant GAB, as agent for Defendants National Union and ***, repeatedly refused to pay for his life-preserving respiratory supplies.

• Because of these unreasonable and outrageous denials, Darien's mother was forced to use her own extremely scarce funds to pay for care that would save her son's life.

• Finally, in late June 1999, the overdue bills that Defendants were obligated but illegitimately refused to pay became so oppressive that Darien's mother was unable to afford them. Only an emergency hearing before a workers' compensation judge alleviated the grave but completely unnecessary threat to Darien Smith's health and life.

• The tortuous campaign described above, which commenced in February 1998 and continued until at least June 1999, constitutes the continuing tort of intentional infliction of emotional distress against

Plaintiff Darien Smith by Defendants ***, National Union, and GAB.

• The tortuous campaign described above constitutes an actionable intentional tort, separate and apart from ***'s obligation, by and through its agents, National Union and GAB to provide and authorize medical benefits for Plaintiff under the Florida Workers Compensation Act.

• This tortuous campaign has resulted in injuries to Plaintiff separate and distinct from the injury he suffered while working at ***, which is subject to and governed by Florida's Workers Compensation Act.

• In conducting this tortuous campaign, Defendants engaged in unlawful, fraudulent, and outrageous conduct. Their conduct goes beyond all bounds of decency and is extreme, outrageous, shocking, atrocious and utterly intolerable in a civilized society.

• Defendants acted with intent to cause Darien Smith severe emotional distress and physical injury or with reckless disregard of the high probability of causing him severe emotional distress and physical injury.

• As a direct result of Defendants' conduct, Darien Smith suffered severe emotional distress, personal injury, damage, and loss.

• As a direct result of Defendants' conduct, Darien Smith was obligated to retain attorneys to represent his interests in this matter, to whom he has agreed to pay reasonable attorneys fees and costs.

- Any and all conditions precedent to bringing this action have been met or waived.

Further counts of intentional infliction of emotional distress included:

- By virtue of his status as a third party beneficiary under these contracts, Defendants ***, National Union, and GAB owed Plaintiff Darien Smith an implied duty to provide him with medical care in good faith.
- By the actions described in paragraphs 25-48 above, Defendants ***, National Union, and GAB breached these duties of implied good faith.
- As a direct result of these breaches, Plaintiff suffered severe emotional distress, personal injury, damage, and loss.
- As a direct result of Defendants' breaches, Darien Smith was obligated to retain attorneys to represent his interests in this matter, to whom he has agreed to pay reasonable attorneys fees and costs.
- Defendants' (National Union and Sedgwick, acting as agents for ***) campaign consisted of manipulating, depriving, denying, and unreasonably delaying medically necessary and life-preserving care to Plaintiff Darien Smith.
- Defendants' (National Union and Sedgwick, acting as agents for ***) campaign was frequently

characterized by an egregious pattern of deceitful, bad-faith extortion and manipulation of Plaintiff Darien Smith. Defendants' pattern was to:

- o deny medically necessary and life-preserving care until legal action was threatened; then
- o agree to provide such care under agreement or other; but then
- o violate such agreements or orders by continuing to delay and deny the provision of care.

• In addition to actions above, Defendants tortuous campaign has extended to knee-jerk, unjustified denials, deprivations, and delays of medically necessary and life-preserving care to which Darien Smith is entitled, including:

- o a retinally-controlled computer to provide Darien with control of the temperature and light in his environment;
- o alternate trained nurses to ensure that Darien has care in the event of an emergency affecting one of his primary nurses;
- o payment of fair market value for nursing care so that Darien could obtain skilled, professional care;
- o brain injury certification to all caregivers, so that they would know how best to preserve Darien's health and life;
- o a badly need psychological care to alleviate Darien's depression;

- o Neuro-optometric evaluation and treatment;
- o A dental evaluation and treatment to address a serious problem involving Darien's tongue;
- o Additional 24-hour on call registered nursing care;
- o A mat table for assisting Darien in transferring out of and into bed;
- o A Spinal Cord Center evaluation;
- o Speech therapist care to enable Darien to communicate more effectively;
- o Nutritionist care to deal with Darien's involuntary bowel movements; and
- o A shower stretcher to allow Darien to shower for the first time since his accident in 1993.

***

Attorney Ted Leopold: Once we got the case filed, there were three or four defendants who each had their own separate attorneys. Like any defendant, they fought, saying that they didn't do anything wrong. They denied everything.

In Florida, before any case can go to trial, there's mandatory mediation, which we actually held in Atlanta with all the parties. Eventually, they were all able to come to an agreement.

The insurance carriers in cases of this type bet on the fact that out of all their bad conduct, only a very, very small percentage of people are like

Linda and will continue to fight. Most, they bet, will give up and move on. At the end of the day, they're dramatically wining, financially and any other way.

I think that a variety of things motivated the worker's comp carrier and other defendants to settle the case with us. First there was the nature of their actions and their outrageous conduct, with Darien's injuries as a result of those actions. I mean, you're not going to get a more sympathetic client in the courtroom than a C-1 ventilator quadriplegic who can only blink his eyes. We put up a timeline, which ran about twenty feet long on a paper printout, of all the things they'd done to this poor kid, and it was a very compelling story.

Had we gone to trial, I think the abuses would have been the key factor in all of this. But it was an accumulation of all the bad acts that ultimately caused the carrier to see that trying this case would expose them. I remember we started the mediation at nine in the morning and didn't settle till seven or eight that evening. This was just last year that we finally settled the case.

Mediation is when both parties give up a little bit in order to take all the risk out of it and get the case resolved. In this matter, the amount we won is confidential but I was very pleased, as I believe Linda and Darien were, with the ultimate result.

In the end, Linda would not stop fighting for her son, and I have no doubt that's the reason why he's alive today. It's rare, with Darien's kind of injury, for the patient to survive. It's amazing.

***

Attorney Jerry Goodmark: For us, this case changed once the liability portion was settled. Then, the insurance company's attitude changed; they began to wonder how they could cooperate and do what we needed them to do. Their attitude has been much better since; not that we haven't had disputes, but it's been much, much better overall.

Darien's worker's comp case has not been settled to date, mainly because worker's comp is different than personal injury in that you don't get just one crack at it. It's a continuing thing. You might go to trial ten times in a worker's comp case if you had multiple issues over the years, as Darien did. There's no one settlement, no one lump sum that the individual gets, unless the parties agree to it.

A judge cannot force either side to settle; he can just rule on the particular medical issues in this case. In fact, we're trying to work out a third settlement in Darien's case, which is indicative of the overarching problem and always has been the main issue: The insurance company has approached this case from the beginning with the attitude that Darien is going to die, so why should they pay him any major lump sum. Darien and his family have proven that that is not going to happen in the timeframe the insurance company thought it would.

I remain the family's attorney in the worker's comp setting. Mr. Leopold is finished with his representation, but there could be another Aguilera suit if it happened again. So far, that kind of conduct has not occurred again. I've moved on now to the point where I'm trying to get Darien everything he needs, as I always have, and I try not to let the bad color what I'm doing now. I try to cooperate with these people if I can.

Chapter 21

I want to be a man that you Would write about a
thousand years from now that they could read about
Your servant of choice in whom you found favor
A man who heard your voice

—4Him, "*A Man You Would Write About*"

Darien, 2009

Because that too had been my hyper-focus for so long, through all the challenges involved in taking care of CJ and Darien, it didn't hit me until about twelve years after Darien's accident, when he finally was stable, that I was lost. I had gotten Darien in a position where I was comfortable that no matter what happened to me, he would be taken care of for the rest of his life. But I woke up one day and realized I didn't have a life. So, I went to the doctor and she informed me, "You've taken yourself out of the equation, and you've got to put yourself back in."

There followed a period when I lost myself, and didn't even know how to begin to get a life. I didn't realize how this situation had affected me mentally and emotionally. One day, I woke up and realized I was dealing with panic attacks and anxiety and depression. I don't know if was in denial and had been able to compartmentalize it so I could deal with what I had in front of me. I've always been the type of person who never panicked in an emergency and always did what I had to do, but later on would have flashbacks.

During those years of struggling with the insurance company, I was just focused on doing what I had to do. The battle was so long and so fierce, I didn't have time to think about myself or what I *needed* and *wanted.* My focus was on getting Darien what *he* needed, because his life literally depended on it. I just did what I had to do.

***

Nurse Carolyn: Linda has calmed down quite a bit. I'm not saying her fears are still not there, because

Darien is her child, but he has come a long way, and so has she. She has been through a lot but has stayed strong, even with the things that were going on with the insurance company. But her quality of life declined to a point where she wasn't going anywhere. She stayed in the house twenty-four/seven and never went anywhere; if she did, she didn't go far and never stayed long because she was always very concerned about Darien's welfare. She couldn't go anywhere without thinking about Darien and what could happen to him, and had a constant feeling of needing to be there with him. She put her children first, always has, both Darien and her other son, CJ.

***

Darien's aunt/head homecare nurse: Me being his auntie and Darien knowing that I'm good at what I do helped build his trust in me. He knew he had somebody with him who had his back and had his care in focus. No matter what else is going on around me, when I'm with Darien, I keep my focus on what he needs to keep the quality of his life going.

***

Now that everything is settled, I can focus on getting a life for myself, and am very excited about that because

I'm still alive at fifty-five. I still have a chance in love and life. I'm open to whatever life has to offer me, which was not even an option in my past, and so I never even considered it.

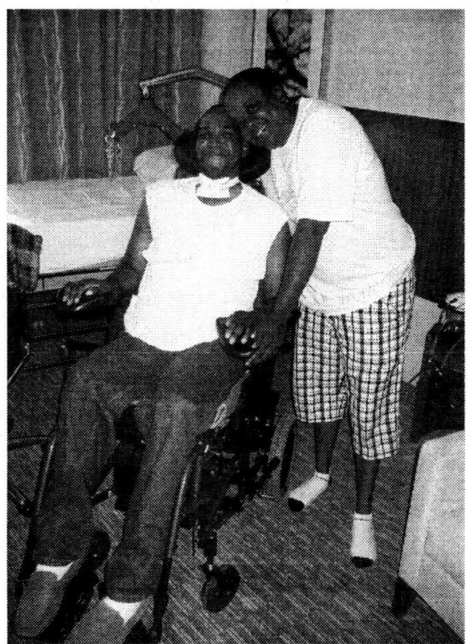

Darien and Auntie Missie

Conclusion

Delight thyself also in the Lord, and he shall give thee the desires of thine heart.

—Psalms 37:4

Darien thirty six years old, 2008

In spite of our recent victories and redemptions in the courts, I do not want to give the impression that going through this experience was easy. There were countless days and nights when we quite literally did not think we were going make it. I could feel death enter my room and my son's room as well, and the weight was so heavy, many times, I wanted to give up. I truly know what it means to be tired of living and afraid to die. I became so tired after defending my son's right to live for fifteen years; that is a long, long, long fight, and the weight of it all at times seemed unbearable.

Whenever I tried to talk to someone, it seemed they didn't understand. Thankfully, Darien and I had a therapist, Dr. Marrinson who was very good at helping Darien with his issues. But how could I tell him how I really felt? I was afraid that if I did, the insurance company would find out how emotionally and mentally tormented I was and say I was incompetent to handle Darien's affairs. That would have been a disaster, so I decided to suffer silently.

Then, there were family and friends who just couldn't get past the material things we had, and thought that was enough to make us happy. I will never understand that, nor will I ever forget it. I believe in forgiveness, but I also believe in awareness. This experience has taught us who our real friends are and the difference between family and relatives—and believe me, there is a difference.

Darien and Dr. Marrinson have made tremendous progress on their own in this respect.

Dr. Marrinson: Darien has relieved some large frustrations in this room.

Darien: I was able to express myself, get back my independence and take some of the frustration out of not being able to speak for myself.

Dr. Marrinson: I didn't have that much in particular in mind as far as where I thought things were going to lead, but the main thing was establishing a communication center and having it act as a lightning rod or a reliever for whatever stresses came up—not just to ventilate, but also to have more control over his own situation.

Darien: To be able to tell him how I really feel, about my anger toward the insurance company, both in terms of how they were treating me and my mother, and that went from anger to hurt.

Dr. Marrinson: And grief. Darien has been able to openly grieve about his loss of ability to function.

Darien: Yes, going from independent to dependant, and learning in these sessions to speak for myself, has helped a little bit, but I'm still confined to that chair. I was angry with the insurance company because they said it was my fault. Everything I have now I had to fight for, and I try not to let my limitations get me down.

Dr. Marrinson: When Darien was able to establish his independence here...

Darien: It gave me my manhood back.

Dr. Marrinson: There have been times when he hasn't wanted any of the people he lives with to see how depressed he gets about being confined, and in those moments, when we're talking, he's been able to express his sadness over that.

Darien: This office is also something of a refuge for me. I feel I can be myself here, Dr. Marrinson. We bonded within a couple of visits and got stronger when I could speak, because it was just him and me. My mom would cry, and that helped to alleviate some of the stress I was feeling when I first started coming to see Dr. Marinson.

Dr. Marrinson: You can't get over something you're still in the middle of. He's still confined to a wheelchair because they ignored his initial injury and pressured him into going back to work, causing paralysis. He'll live with that the rest of his life, and every day he is reminded of it, so he can't move past it. He can grow into a better relationship with it instead of being a helpless victim. This change in his relationship to his paralysis did not begin in here when we started working together; it began the day he was paralyzed in his walk with God. That has been the primary way in which Darien has overcome the crushing blow that life dealt him and the evil of putting money over human life that the insurance company put him through. Most people would feel trapped by that in a way that could crush their spirit, and they would end up on a lot of heavy medication. I have a lot of people I see every day, not as injured as Darien, who are miserable, bitter, defeated, and feel their injuries haves ruined their lives. In contrast, from the beginning of his paralysis, Darien recognized that God was there for him and used his faith and his relationship with God to get stronger in his dependence on God's grace and mercy, and to fall into His arms, to get the comfort and relief from the emotional pain, rage and outrage. There's nothing quite as debilitating to the human spirit as helpless outrage over having evil done to you.

Darien: I've never gotten angry at God. I've always felt this was for a reason. That's why I never got upset with God. I always ask God to let me be a sacrifice, holy and acceptable.

Dr. Marrinson: This has been Darien's way of responding to this injury since the day it happened.

He didn't need anybody like me to get him right in that. Our relationship helped it along.

Darien: So Dr. Marrinson has been helpful with managing everything outside of that center I already had with God, and I hope that this book will be an instrument in the service of the sacrifice that I have vowed to make for God within the boundaries of that sacrifice.

Dr. Marrinson: When most people see Darien for the first time, they're horrified, and Darien's smile is the spirit transcending that horror.

Darien: I'm not aware of the positive feelings my smile inspires in others, whether working on my behalf. I'm human, and I have bad days and good days. Every Sunday I go to a nondenominational church called Free Spirit. I enjoy the sermons by Pastor Foster and have been attending this church for a little over a year. Psalms 91:5 is my favorite verse. It reads: "Thou shall not be afraid for the terror by night, nor for the arrow that flyeth by day." It makes me fearless of evil. That has been a constant for me throughout everything, even before this happened.

Dr. Marrinson: There are periods of time, especially

during fights with the insurance company over medical needs or while watching his mother break down in tears over the stress of dealing with them, when his outrage has been so overwhelming, it was difficult for him to smile.

Darien: Yes.

Dr. Marrinson: And during those times, when his normal, natural, human, intense emotional reactions to the shit that hits the fan occasionally with his case, when those emotions are overwhelming, it has been a struggle for him to feel God's presence in his heart while he's praying, and feeling God's presence in his heart when he prays is the primary method by which Darien has managed to overcome the horror and grief of what's happened to him, and still be able to shine through that outrage.

Darien: Keeping faith has been challenging at times.

Dr. Marrinson: That sacrifice is the point of this, that he can be an example to others in overcoming the adversity in their own lives.

Darien: That has been as hard for me to realize as it would be for anyone who reads my story.

Dr. Marrinson: Anyone who is open to the love of God, which we feel when our hearts open up to His spirit and the soul that God breathes into us, they have the potential to overcome what Darien has.

Darien: Right. In church, sometimes I hear something new, but more than anything it's a reaffirmation of my faith.

Dr. Marrinson: With Darien's struggle to keep his spirit from being crushed by turning to God for help, I'm not at all sure that that struggle is more difficult than the garden-variety hardships everyday people have to keep their spirits strong. The extent of the hardship—say, being in Darien's position versus the everyday stresses of being a doctor in America in 2009—is not necessarily the extent of the difficulty sustaining the spirit. One of the things that needs to come out that Darien has experienced is God's helping hand, and the hardship has opened up his heart even more and made it easier for him to be helped by those around him. This book is an invitation for readers to look at what God has accomplished for Darien.

Darien: To never give up, and to understand through my example that if I can do it, you can do it.

Dr. Marrinson: The "do it" part, what we all need to do, is in the course of daily living, our spirits can get crushed almost every day by things we see in the human condition and life on Earth. One way or another, we're all going to be upset by things we encounter in life. There's no escaping that, and that's not cause for despair; it may actually be what its all about. We must not be broken by the hardships of our particular lives.

Darien: Sometimes God will take you take you around the storm, and sometimes he'll take you through the storm…

***

We are not bitter because of our experience; it really made us stronger and more determined to succeed at what we're striving for, which is getting Darien help so that one day he will have a second chance at life. This experience has taught us that we are all free to live life no matter how physically, mentally or emotionally challenged we are. We all have choices about how we want to live our lives. I chose to stay home for fourteen years to protect my son from outsiders trying to prematurely take his life. Darien wanted to live, and I wanted him to live, and our collective will has proven more powerful than any of those negative forces. I have no regrets, and would do it all over again if I had to. It came so easy to me because I love my son unconditionally, in spite of his many medical issues that everyone else felt made his fight a lost cause. For our family, giving up was never an option.

In all of the circumstances in our lives, we are able to make lemonade out of our lemons—that's just how we live. If someone gets in trouble, we don't beat them down or turn our backs. We have truly unconditional love. We are so blessed to have had so many people in our lives to pray for and support us. We will always be eternally grateful.

Unfortunately, we were not able to name all the doctors, nurses, family members and friends who were there for us, but we truly appreciate their prayers and compassion, which have helped sustain us on this journey. I will never forget the day I walked into a men's store to buy Darien some clothes to wear to church. The owner gave me a cassette tape about healing, and Darien has listened to that tape for over ten years. We want to thank Open Word Ministries in Atlanta, Georgia, and pastor Gary Taylor, who has never met us, but his praise and worship service CD still keeps our faith strong. We believe that God can heal in any manner He chooses.

I am an active supporter of stem-cell research to help victims of paralysis. To those of you who are opposed to stem-cell research, I ask you not to judge too harshly. If you can, just imagine what it would be like for Darien and others like him to have the opportunity to hug a family member or friends, to breath on his own again or even just walk down the street and pick a rose again for his mother. Yes, we are desperate for another chance at life for our loved ones, but only because we love them and want the best for them in life. We know God is sovereign, and we will take a miracle any way God sees fit to give it to us, whether it's supernatural or through medical science. To God be the glory.

***

> Nurse Carolyn: Looking to the future, I think Darien looks forward to going back to school. He wants to be a motivational speaker and tell his story. Because he is a Christian, he has a humble spirit and just wants to help others overcome the types of obstacles he's had to overcome in his own life.
>
> I didn't know what I was walking into, but looking back, I don't have any regrets about any of it, absolutely not. I don't have one regret. I think it's been very rewarding, and we have had our ups and downs, but we maintain and we put aside our differences because it's not about us—it's

about Darien. That's why I'm here; Darien is the main reason, only him. I love everybody here just like they are my family, and I will be right there whenever he gets up and walks again for the first time. I'll be right there with him.

***

Darien's aunt/head homecare nurse: Because Darien's injury was at the brain stem, he would be a good candidate for stem-cell treatment. Every year, he's making progress and can make his fingers and little toes move. What keeps me moving along is God's promise to Darien, God's promise to my sister and God's promise to me, and I feel that no matter what circumstances we are faced with, we have to hold on to what God promised.

I know that in every situation, God allows you to be in it and keeps you in it because He wants to be glorified. That's what I see: the glory of God. That's what helps me hold on. I see the hand of God over Darien's life, because he's better than he was before. He's not like he was when he came home from Shepherd. Right there, you see God's glory. I'm just holding on to the promise that Darien will walk again. That's what keeps me going.

***

Though we are now blessed with financial stability, we

will never put money or things before God or people. There were some who couldn't see our struggles because they were looking at the material things God has so graciously given us. To those who cruelly ask, "Wouldn't you would rather have your son walking than all the material things that you have?" I say, "Keep living. The best is yet to come."

I believe we will have it all. Thank God for Christopher Reeve and everyone who is doing research on stem cells to help people like Darien. A big shout out to our president, Barak Obama, for lifting the ban on stem-cell research. In the words of Winston Churchill, never, never give up!

Now marks a new chapter in our lives. We still have one more big hurdle, and that's getting Darien out of his wheelchair. If it should not happen, no one will be able to look back and say we didn't give it all we had.

I have found myself once again and am ready to live life to the fullest. Darien, of course, wishes he was not in this situation, but since he is, he is determined to live his life to the best of his ability. We have learned so much from this experience: patience, which ranks high on the list, faith, love, how to conquer fear and how to survive the worst of times when it seems all hope is gone. You can be strong if you choose to be; remember, you always have a choice. Always choose to stand, come in fighting and go out fighting—that's what Darien is consistently doing.